The
ART & CRAFT
of
DOUGH

The
ART & CRAFT
of
DOUGH

JOANNA JONES

PREMIER EDITIONS

To those two great scholars — my sister,
Sally Wathen, and the Governor — with love.

ACKNOWLEDGEMENT
My thanks to Maisie Blackburn and her staff, Blackburns,
Cake Decorations and Craft Equipment, 108 Alexandra
Drive, Surbiton, Surrey KT5 9AG, who are extremely
helpful and will usually send equipment to any destination.

Published in 1995 by Premier Editions
an imprint of Merehurst Limited, Ferry House, 51–57 Lacy Road,
Putney, London SW15 1PR

Copyright © Merehurst Limited 1995
ISBN 1-897730-26-8

A catalogue record of this book is available from the
British Library.

Edited by Bridget Jones and Heather Dewhurst
Designed by Maggie Aldred
Photography by James Duncan

Typeset by J&L Composition Ltd, Filey, North Yorkshire
Colour separation and printing by
Toppan, Singapore

CONTENTS

Introduction 6

Equipment, Recipes and Basic Techniques 8

Painting and Problem Solving 20

Baskets and Bowls 24

Garlands and Wreaths 34

Characters 46

Houses and Cottages 72

Decorated Initials 87

Christmas Decorations 97

Table Decorations 114

Romantic Messages 127

Templates 138

Marketing and Selling 140

Index 144

INTRODUCTION

When I first saw a piece of dough modelling I could not believe that something so appealing and apparently so enduring could be made from what was, basically, food. I was captivated by a gorgeous little rustic doll that a friend had hanging in her kitchen – it had been left mainly dough coloured, with just its rosy cheeks and some parts of the clothing painted. It was charming.

The doll was a gift brought from some remote part of the country and, needless to say, no-one knew how it was made. As an artist, nothing gets my creative juices flowing more quickly than the prospect of working with new materials, so, totally inspired, I called into the library on my way home confident of finding a book that would reveal the secret of the dough. There was no such book – not in the library, the book shop nor the craft shop; not under the counter nor on the black market; not on friends' bookshelves;

not even to be purchased by post! I am known for my tenacity and I wanted to know how to model dough. I wanted to know exactly what was in the recipe, whether it was cooked and, if so, for how long and at what temperature. What type of paint was on it? Did it need varnishing?

I began a quest for information and no-one was spared from interrogation. Casual conversations started at parties, on trains or in bus queues were gradually worked around to the subject of dough modelling and its complexities but all to no avail. If anyone knew anything, they were keeping very quiet about it. At the end of two years of dedicated questioning, I was none the wiser about the secret practices of dough modellers except for one slender clue: there had been several references to pieces seen abroad, with particular mention of pieces from America, Germany and various Scandinavian countries. I

therefore decided to target people with foreign accents and – although it slowed down my investigations considerably and, as you might imagine, led to some bizarre misunderstandings – this eventually paid off.

My family had long since closed ranks against my obsession and banned any public manifestations of it in their presence. Despite this, I had arranged our Christmas shopping so that a bit of dough research in Harrods' book department went almost unnoticed. As I managed to conduct what was surely a fruitless search among the craft books, I overhead the remnants of a conversation and picked up an unmistakeable American accent. I turned to see an exasperated American man darting between the bookshelves and a large lady in a wheelchair. He was on the point of exploding as his latest offering, a weighty craft book, was again rejected. 'The fact of the matter is,' he hissed, 'you've done every craft known to man.'

This lady had all the attributes of a perfect interviewee – she was American, she had 'done every craft known to man' and she was unable to escape. I seized my chance and made general conversation on a diversity of crafts, such as American quilting and British barge painting, before asking her The Question. 'Have you ever done any dough modelling?' I tried to make it sound as casual as the rest of the conversation but I could hardly contain my excitement and the words seemed to hang in the air for hours before she answered: 'Heck, yes, masses of it'.

I scrabbled in my bag for an old envelope and a pencil as my new-found friend looked across to her husband, who had defected to the section on sports books, settled herself back in her chair, then proceeded to enlighten me on the alchemy that transformed mere dough into an art.

EQUIPMENT, RECIPES AND BASIC TECHNIQUES

After my magical encounter with the American lady, I rushed home and started making dough immediately before I could forget anything. Apart from the basic ingredients of flour and salt, the only other equipment I had then, and for many years, was a sharp knife, a rolling pin, a pair of nail scissors, a garlic press and a pair of eyebrow tweezers. With this motley collection, occasionally supplemented with a cocktail stick (toothpick) or an old retractable ballpoint pen, I made literally hundreds of dough models in dozens of different designs. I also sold them, demonstrated the techniques, gave talks and had started teaching Adult Education Classes when I had my second encounter of a dough kind . . .

One of my students was a pastry cook. After listening patiently to my description of how to cut out and make a flower with a pair of nail scissors, he asked me politely if I would mind if he used his sugarcraft cutters instead. I had never heard of sugarcraft and had no idea that shops existed solely to sell equipment designed to make modelling

in sugar, and consequently in dough, much easier. These exciting specialist shops have greatly increased in number – now almost every large town has one and, I warn you, they lure dough modellers and their cheque books like magnets. Many specialist outlets also provide a mail order service.

After a hard day's dough modelling, it

is very tempting to throw all your cutters into their box and put your feet up but try to get into the habit of washing all your equipment promptly after use. Unfortunately, the high salt content of the dough will cause metal tools, especially scissors, to rust if they are not washed and dried after use.

Dough Recipes

Now that dough modelling is so popular, there are almost as many different recipes as books. The recipe I scribbled down in Harrods was extremely basic and consisted of flour, salt and water. I used the recipe exclusively for many years and have modified it only slightly of late, adding a little oil in an effort to alleviate the dough modeller's curse . . . cracking!

I cannot stress enough how important it is to knead the dough thoroughly, but I am also well aware that, despite zealous kneading, the demon cracks can still appear. Hours after the piece has been baked you may actually hear the dough cracking.

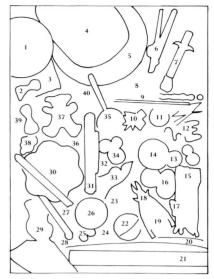

1 Rimless dish **2** Yellow stamens
3 Net **4** Dish with rim **5** Lattice
cutter **6** Garlic press **7** Clay gun
and pattern discs **8** Calyx cutters,
daffodil cutters and little bird
cutter **9** Artist's paint brush and
wooden skewer **10** Cocktail sticks
11 Carnation cutter **12** Large letter
cutter **13** Ivy leaf cutters **14** Cloves
15 Modelling tools **16** Leaf cutters
17 Blossom plunger cutters
18 Wire cutters **19** Primrose
cutters **20** Floristry wire **21** Plastic
ruler **22** Fluted cooky cutter
23 Hair pins **24** Holly leaf cutters
25 Nail scissors **26** Poppy seeds
27 Plastic tweezers **28** Sharp knife
29 Wallpaper paste **30** Flower-
shaped china palette and paint
brushes **31** Rolling pin **32** Old
retractable ballpoint pen **33** Bird
cutter **34** Daisy cutter **35** Fine
sieve **36** Butterfly cutter **37** Teddy
bear cutter **38** Brooch backs
39 Black stamens **40** Round rose
cutters and Briar rose cutters.

*Equipment is available from sugarcraft
suppliers or artists' suppliers. Metal cutters
give a cleaner cut than plastic cutters.*

·BASIC DOUGH·

*225g (8oz/2 cups) plain (all
purpose) flour
100g (4oz/½ cup) salt
2 teaspoons cooking oil*

1   Thoroughly mix the flour and salt in a bowl and then add the oil and 100ml (4 fl oz/½ cup) water. Stir the water and oil into the flour mixture and start to bind the ingredients into a dough. Discard the spoon at this point and mix the dough with your hand, adding more water gradually by sprinkling it into the mix with your fingertips. By adding the water drip by drip, you will know the instant the dough is ready. It should be firm enough not to stick to your hands but not so dry that it is crumbly.

2   Turn the dough out onto a smooth surface and knead it for at least 10 minutes, until it is smooth, pliable and very slightly warm.

Note   The Basic Dough is a salt dough. Where a quantity of Basic Dough is listed, be sure to use the above recipe, not the Bread Dough (below).

·PASTE DOUGH·

This mixture will seem slightly sticky while you are making it but it should become smooth and warm when kneaded. It has a texture which is a little more elastic than the Basic Dough.

*45g (1½oz) wallpaper paste
375g (12oz) plain (all-purpose)
white flour*

*375g (12oz) salt
185ml (6 fl oz) cold water*

1   Mix the wallpaper paste with water, if necessary, following the manufacturer's instructions and observe any suggested standing time.

2   Mix the flour and salt in a bowl, then add the wallpaper paste. Proceed as for Basic Dough, step 2.

·BREAD DOUGH·

The ingredients for bread dough are totally different from those in salt dough and the result is a dough of such a fine texture that it is possible to make flowers with petals as delicate as porcelain. As it is so delicate, this dough is only really suitable for making small objects; although in theory you could make it up in large quantities and use it in thick portions to make something big, in practice you would really be defeating the object of using this recipe. Larger pieces look more attractive and are easier to make using salt dough.

The first stages of kneading Bread Dough.

Both types of dough require kneading; unfortunately the bread dough has to be kneaded for 15–20 minutes, during which time your hands are in such a mess that you really need to plan ahead before you start.

Answering telephone calls or calls of nature are definitely not recommended while the dough is in its early stages!

*100g (4oz) day-old white bread
without crusts
3 tablespoons P.V.A. glue
1 tablespoon white acrylic paint
1 teaspoon glycerine (glycerol)*

1   Break the bread into small pieces about the size of sugar cubes and place them in a bowl. Add the rest of the ingredients, wiping the remains of the sticky glue and paint off the spoon each time with a piece of the bread.

2   Bind the mixture together by stirring it with a spoon until it forms a ball. Scoop up the dough with your hands and knead it between your palms for 15–20 minutes. Your hands will be completely coated with white paint and glue at first, but persevere and very soon you will notice that the ball of dough will be growing smoother and your hands will be cleaner.

3   If after 30 minutes the dough is either far too wet or too dry, add more breadcrumbs to wet dough or a little more glycerine to dry dough and continue to knead.

4   Wrap the ball of dough in cling film (plastic wrap) and put it into an airtight container in the refrigerator until you need to use it. It will keep for months if stored in this way.

Note When you have taken the dough from the bowl, make sure that you fill the bowl with water and place the spoon in it, otherwise the mixture will have dried hard by the time you are free to do the washing up.

After many years of teaching dough modelling, I know that at some time during the kneading exercise you are more than likely to doubt me, but have faith . . . If you persevere, you *will* end up with a beautiful ball of smooth white dough, which will be slightly softer than plasticine.

KNEADING BREAD DOUGH

Scoop the bread dough out of the mixing bowl as soon as the ingredients form a ball. There is absolutely no point in trying to mix it in the container, as all you will be doing is spreading the rapidly drying paint and glue around the side of the bowl.

Knead the dough by pressing it first into one palm and then into the other. Be firm about this action and do not spread the dough by stroking the fingers of one hand against the palm of the other. If you are kneading bread dough properly you should actually feel the effect on your pectoral muscles and this exercise might even develop your chest!

As you work, the glue and paint on your hands will gradually be taken up by the ball of dough, which will become very smooth and supple. When kneaded sufficiently there should be absolutely no sign of any bread.

QUANTITIES

Some projects call for $\frac{1}{2}$ quantity Bread Dough, but it is not worth making less than the amount given above; just store the leftover dough in the refrigerator ready for making another model.

DRYING

Bread dough takes about 6 hours to dry at room temperature; the exact length of time depends on the individual pieces.

Colouring Bread Dough

Take a small chunk of bread dough and flatten it out slightly. Squeeze a little gouache or water colour paint onto the dough and then fold the dough over it and knead it in. Continue kneading until the paint is well distributed and the colour is even, adding more paint or dough until the colour is right.

This is an undeniably messy business and you may well be tempted to leave the dough white and paint it at the end. This is not always a good idea because, although you invariably paint over the coloured dough, there are nooks and crannies that you cannot reach without smudging something else, so it helps if it is almost the same colour and you can leave it unpainted.

Colouring the dough also seems to refine it, making it less coarse.

·EGG GLAZE·

Egg glaze gives salt dough a lovely golden colour if you paint it on before baking. To make a glaze beat an egg with

1 tablespoon water. Do not glaze dough that you intend to paint later as it will prevent the paint from flowing on easily. If you require a really deep colour, you may repeat the application of glaze every 20 minutes or so throughout the cooking time.

Salt Dough Modelling Techniques

KNEADING SALT DOUGH

As soon as as all the ingredients are well bound together, tip the ball of dough out onto a lightly floured smooth surface. Take hold of the dough with both hands, then press down and push it away from you with the base of your palms.

Alternate this action with a sideways folding movement to keep the ball of dough roughly the same size and shape as it is kneaded. Continue kneading for at least 10 minutes by which time the dough should be smooth and very slightly warm.

It is essential to knead the dough firmly and for the recommended time to avoid problems when modelling.

ROLLING ROPES

Roll a piece of well-kneaded salt dough into a rough sausage shape on a lightly floured board. Place the fingers of both hands together in the middle of the sausage and work them out towards the ends, rolling the dough backwards and forwards. Repeat this procedure until the rope is the required length and thickness. By using your fingers rather than the palms of your hands, you exert less pressure on the dough and have more control, and therefore your rope is more likely to be of an even thickness.

Dough which has not been thoroughly kneaded splits when it is rolled into a rope.

MAKING A TWIST

Lay two ropes of dough of the same length and thickness side by side. Starting in the centre, twist them around each other, then work outwards, first to one end and then to the other. Fix the ropes together at both ends. By working from the middle outwards, you are less likely to stretch the dough and end up with a twist which has one thin end and one thick end.

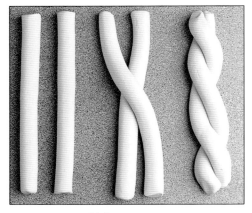

Making a twist.

WEAVING DOUGH

Roll out a large piece of dough to the required thickness. Using a well-floured plastic ruler and a sharp knife, cut the dough into even-sized strips. Most complete bowls and baskets take approximately ten strips.

Place two strips of dough one over the other in the form of a cross. Lay a third strip parallel to the bottom strip and over the second one. Weave a fourth strip over the last strip and under the bottom first strip. Continue weaving dough strips in this way, alternating vertical and horizontal strips, until you have a section large enough for your project. Keep checking to see whether you have woven enough strips as you go. It is easier to weave strips under if you fold the top strips back and then replace them afterwards.

Weaving dough: it is easier to weave strips under if you fold top strips back.

There is not usually any need to fix the strips to each other with water, but it is sometimes necessary when you are working on a steep-sided bowl or dish.

MAKING HAIR

Dough is extruded through a garlic press, clay gun or a fine sieve, such as a nylon tea strainer, to make hair. Whichever method you use, try to give your figures a recognizable style, rather than leaving the dough in a tangled mess, and avoid wispy arrangements or stray locks as these tend to break off.

Garlic press Fill the press with a smooth ball of dough, then push it through the holes. If the resultant strands are long enough, cut them off using a sharp knife. If you want longer hair, re-charge the press with dough, before cutting the first batch off and push some more through.

Wet the head and then, transferring single strands of hair on some well-floured tweezers, gradually build up the hair style.

Clay gun There are two or three different types of clay gun available from sugarcraft shops. They all work along similar lines and may be used for a variety of different effects. To make hair, fit one of the sieve-like discs into the end of the gun and load the tube with slightly dampened dough.

Pull the trigger to push strands of dough out onto a lightly floured board. Then use floured plastic tweezers to pick up little clumps of hair and transfer these to the dampened head pressing firmly into place on the head.

Clay-gun hair is usually much finer than garlic-press hair and with care it can be extruded in waves, straight onto the head. It can also be coaxed into curls after it has been arranged on the head by using a cocktail stick (toothpick) or modelling tool.

Fine sieve As this method gives a compact effect, I use it to make hair for short, male styles, for little dolls and for a permed effect.

Pushing dough through a fine sieve to make hair.

Soften the dough slightly with a little water and, using the back of a wooden spoon, push it through the sieve. The longer you work away with the spoon, the longer the hair on the other side of the sieve will grow, but as this method gives a very compact effect it is best to reserve it for short styles.

Remove the hair from the back of the sieve with a sharp knife and transfer it directly to the head.

Curls For creatures such as cherubs, who simply must have big fat curls, the only solution is to roll them by hand.

Make several very small tapering ropes about 12mm ($\frac{1}{2}$in) in length and, starting at one end, roll each rope into a coil. Dot these all over the head at different angles; I usually reserve one, which is coming slightly uncurled, for the forehead.

MODELLING ARMS AND HANDS
Lay two suitable ropes of dough side by side on a floured board. Flatten the ends closest to you with a finger, then use a sharp knife to cut a small triangle of dough from the inside edge of each of the flattened pieces to represent the space between the thumb and the first finger.

Make three small cuts along the bottom edge of each piece to represent the fingers and trim these to the appropriate lengths. Using the sharp knife or a damp paint brush, carefully round the ends of the fingers and thumbs to give them shape.

While the arms are still laying side by side, trim the tops of them diagonally so that the two diagonals form a 'V'; these slanting ends will eventually fit on either side of the body.

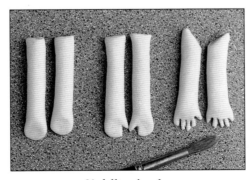

Modelling hands.

MAKING LEGS AND FEET
To make legs and feet that are wearing boots or shoes, lay two suitable ropes of dough together on a floured board. Leave the bottom ends of these ropes untrimmed so that they retain their rounded appearance.

Lay a finger across one of the ropes, about 12mm ($\frac{1}{2}$in) from the rounded end, and roll the rope very gently to make a slight indentation. Dab a spot of water on the indentation and then bend the rounded end up at right angles to form a foot. Make the other foot in the same way.

If you wish to give the appearance of boots, fix a very thin rope of dough around each leg, just above the ankle or halfway up the calf.

To make legs with bare feet, lay the ropes side by side as before, but trim both bottom ends diagonally so that together they form a 'V'. Make four small cuts along the diagonal edges to represent toes and round each toe off, either with a sharp knife or a damp brush. As bare feet are generally used on flying angels or cherubs I do not usually bend them at the ankle, but if you want that effect treat them as above.

While the legs are still together, trim the top ends diagonally so that together they form a 'V'; these diagonals fit on either side of the body.

MAKING A BOW
Cut two long, narrow strips of dough. Cut a quarter of the length from one and cut the other in half diagonally. Take the diagonally cut pieces and

13

notch both the straight ends with a knife before fixing the diagonal ends together on the model.

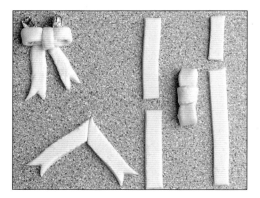

Making a bow.

Loop both ends of the longest remaining piece towards the middle and fix together in the centre. Wrap the last short piece around the middle to represent the knot and fix together at the back. Arrange the bow in the middle of the ribbon tails. Fill the loops with some crushed silver foil, if necessary, to support their shape during baking.

Note You may like to use a plastic strip cutter instead of a knife to get all the strips looking exactly the same. These are available in sugarcraft shops.

MAKING A FRILL
Use a fluted round cutter of a suitable size to cut out a circle of thinly rolled dough. Use a smaller round cutter to remove the centre of the fluted circle.

Using a cocktail stick (toothpick) like a very small rolling pin, roll out each of the flutes around the circle, with a gentle rocking motion. Flour the cocktail stick repeatedly while you work.

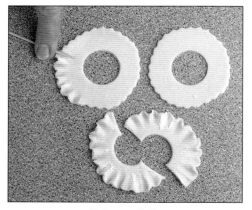

Making a frill.

When you have frilled the complete ring, cut it into the required lengths.

MAKING A SITTING CAT
Make two slim ropes of dough for the front legs and lay them side by side on a floured board. Make three small cuts along the front edge of both to represent the toes. Round each of these individually with a damp paint brush. Trim the other end of each leg diagonally and fix together with a little water.

Place a small pear-shaped piece of dough on top of the legs, with the tapered end facing the front, so that about half the legs are still protruding. Make a small ball of dough for the head and add a very small triangular wedge of dough to make the nose.

Add two very small flattened balls of dough close to the nose, to represent whisker pads. Fix the head in place on the body of the cat. Make two pointed ears by cutting a small circle with a small round cutter and quartering it. Flatten two of these quarters a little and fit them to the top of the cat's head. Fix a thin

tapering rope of dough on the rear of the cat and then curl it around the body to make the tail.

Note If you want to attach the cat's head at a particularly awkard angle, using water alone might not be enough to hold it. Take a short length of wire and push half of it into the head and the other half into the body to reinforce the join.

MAKING A BUTTERFLY
Using the butterfly cutter, stamp the shape out of thinly rolled dough and lay it on a lightly floured board. Use a cocktail stick (toothpick) to flute the outside edges of the wings, as when making a frill, then fix the butterfly on the project with a little water. Roll a very small cigar-shaped body and fix this between the two wings.

Wet the sides of the body a little and push the wings up so that they adhere to it. If the wings droop, then support them in an upright position by tucking two small rolls of foil underneath them during baking. Trim two black stamens to the right length and push these into the front of the body to represent antennae.

To make a very small butterfly, cut out two heart shapes and trim off the pointed ends. Stick these wings on either side of a small cigar-shaped body and support them with foil if necessary. Small butterflies look better if you paint their antennae in front of their heads on the main dough model after it is baked.

MODELLING BIRDS
Doves Take a small ball of well-kneaded dough and pull out one side

slightly. Model this into a rounded head with a pinched-in neck and a small beak.

Flatten the other end of the dough into a fan-shaped tail, pinching it in at the base. Tip the tail up slightly and make three or four small cuts along the edge to represent tail feathers.

Use a small leaf cutter to make two wings and feather these with the back of a knife. Finish using a cocktail stick (toothpick) to indent two eyes in the dough.

Robin Make the head, wings and beak as for the dove, but instead of making a fan-shaped tail, pull the dough out to a point to suggest long tail feathers.

Pigeon Start the pigeon in a similar way to the dove, but make the head smaller and the body streamlined, ending in a tail like the one on the robin.

If the pigeon is very big, make thin wings with a leaf cutter, but if it is quite small it will look better with painted wings, added after baking.

MAKING A TEDDY

Model two short, thin ropes of dough with feet as for the Victorian Girl, see page 46. Trim the other ends of the legs diagonally.

For the body, mould a small ball of dough into an egg shape and flatten it slightly where the arms and legs are going to be attached. Sit the body up on a baking sheet or in position on a model and attach the legs to the appropriate flattened areas, pressing into position. Make two more thin, short ropes of dough for arms and cut a little notch in one end of each to represent thumbs.

Making a teddy.

Trim the other ends diagonally and fit these in place on the body. Arrange the paws against the body.

For the head, mould a small ball of dough into a rounded pyramid shape. Take the more pointed end for a snout and fix a small triangular piece of dough on the end for a nose. Flatten two very small balls of dough and fix these close to the nose to represent whisker pads. Make two more small balls of dough into small saucer-shaped ears by pressing with the rounded end of a modelling tool. Fix these in position and add a bow on the neck.

MAKING ROSES AND ROSEBUDS

To make roses and rosebuds, I generally use the two smallest cutters in a small set of round cutters; the set is sometimes sold as a 'Briar Rose' set.

Cut out two small circles and two larger ones from thinly rolled dough. Cut all the circles in half and flatten them slightly with the ball of your thumb or fingertip to make the edges as thin as possible.

Take one of the smaller semi-circles

and, starting at one corner, carefully roll the dough into a coil to resemble the centre of a rose. Fix the end by dabbing a little water on it. You may leave some pieces at this stage to represent rosebuds.

Dampen the longest edges of the three small semi-circles with water before wrapping them evenly around the central bud, overlapping them to make them fit. At this stage the roses may be used as small flowers if you prefer. Add the final four large semi-circles by wrapping them around the bud to make full-blown roses.

MAKING LEAVES WITHOUT CUTTERS

Press a small fresh leaf into the rolled-out dough, then use nail scissors to cut around the impression which it leaves. This will give realistic veining and works wonderfully with short and odd-shaped leaves, such as those from primroses.

Long tapering leaves, like those on daffodils, are best made by cutting

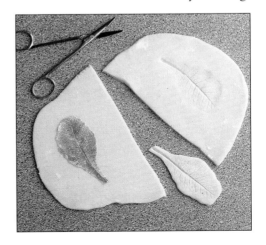

Pressing a fresh primrose leaf into dough to leave an impression which may be cut out.

them out freehand with a sharp knife, then adding a long central vein afterwards. If they do go a bit crooked, it doesn't matter as this only adds to the sense of realism.

VEINING LEAVES

There are cutters available for making a wide variety of leaves, but the most useful is the rose leaf which can usually double up for other types.

To vein the rose leaf, use the back of a knife to mark a central vein and then add four or five pairs of smaller veins coming from it.

Leaves like ivy and holly have such distinctive shapes that you really have to buy the proper cutter. Use the back of a knife to give both of them a central vein only. The ivy cutter will also double for a grape vine leaf.

MAKING FLOWERS WITH A PRIMROSE CUTTER

The primrose cutter is another very versatile piece of equipment which can be used to make a variety of other flowers.

Primrose or Primula Cut the shape out of thinly rolled dough and fix the flower in position, then make a hole in the middle with the pointed end of a modelling tool. This will give a deep, wide hole which will look quite realistic when painted.

Christmas Rose Cut out a flower and lay it in the palm of your hand, then gently press each petal with the rounded end of a modelling tool to

thin and slightly cup the petals. Fix the flower in position and fill the centres with five shortened stamens.

Dog Rose Make the flowers as for Christmas rose, but use slightly longer stamens. The main difference is in the painting.

DAISIES

Daisy cutters usually come in sets of three, so you can make anything from a small daisy to a large Marguerite.

Lay the cut-out flower on a thin piece of foam rubber and press each petal with the small leaf-shaped end of a modelling tool. Pull the tool back slightly as you do this and it will have the effect of curving the edges of each petal towards each other. Place a small flattened ball of dough in the centre of the daisy and prick this all over with a cocktail stick.

MAKING CARNATIONS

Using a carnation cutter set, cut one of each size of circles from thinly rolled dough and lay them on a well-floured board. Use a sharp knife to make three short cuts in each of the flutes on every circle. Use a well-floured wooden skewer to roll out each flute with a short rocking movement to make them slightly ragged and frilled like the edges of fresh carnation petals.

Dampen the middle of each circle, then stack them with the largest at the bottom and the smallest on top. Pick up all the petals together and pinch them together from underneath so that they make a flower shape before you fix them in position.

Making a Carnation Without Cutters Cut out a circle of dough with a small round fluted cutter, then snip the flutes and roll them using a well-floured skewer in the same way as above.

Fold the circle in half, then in half again to make a triangle or wedge shape with all the frills at the top. Trim off the pointed end of the triangle and fix the

Making carnations: the cut-out shapes are frilled and stacked, the skewer may be pushed through the centre before pinching the petals together at the back.

flower in position before carefully opening out and arranging the petals to look more realistic.

MOULDING VIOLETS

Fit a small ball of dough over the pointed end of a skewer to cover the top 6mm ($\frac{1}{4}$ in) without breaking through the dough.

Make four or five cuts in the bottom edge of the dough to make three or four strips and one wider one. With the dough still on the end of the skewer, carefully lift

Making violets.

each of the strips and press them between your finger and thumb, bending them outwards like petals at the same time.

Remove the violet from the skewer and shape the petals a little more with your fingers before arranging it on your model.

MAKING DAFFODILS
It is best to work directly on the model as a dough daffodil is impossible to pick up once it has been made; it will fall apart very easily. Using a daffodil cutter set, take the smaller of the two petal cutters and use it to cut five petals from thinly rolled dough. Arrange these in a circle with their ends touching in the middle.

Cut out the trumpet. Working on a floured board, make several small cuts along the longest edge with a knife, then use a well floured wooden skewer to roll the edge gently so that the dough becomes more splayed and ragged. Carefully roll the trumpet around the skewer so that the short edges meet and fix them

together with a little water applied with your fingers. Pinch the unfrilled end of the tube together and fix the trumpet into the middle of the petal circle.

Making Daffodils Without Cutters
Daffodils can also be made without cutters, simply by making a cardboard template for the petals and cutting the regular piece straight instead of curved. It is advisable to use nail scissors to cut the dough.

MAKING HANGING HOOKS
The most successful hanging hooks are made from traditional hairpins. Trim them to length, as necessary for your

Making daffodils.

project, using wire cutters. The trimmings from the straight-sided pins may be bent into hooks as well.

Painting and Varnishing

Painting brings dough models to life and makes them look interesting. Unfortu-

nately, most of the models you see for sale have been painted with unsuitable paints and the results are crude. Treat yourself to professional paints and brushes and give up any ideas of a trial run with the children's paint box and a cosmetic brush!

You could use two or three old saucers instead of a palette, but a 'Chrysanthemum' palette is the most useful and china will not stain in the same way as plastic. Paints, brushes, palettes and spirit-based acrylic varnish are all available in the art shop, but go to a do-it-yourself store to purchase oil-based polyurethane varnish.

Absorbent paper is handy for wiping brushes and to lay your model on while you are painting. I also have a sharp craft knife and some cotton buds so that I can erase the inevitable mistake, wiping it off with the bud or scraping it off with the knife.

For bread dough you will also need a chunk of polystyrene (styrofoam) of the kind used for packaging or flower arranging and hand cream which should be as non sticky as possible.

PAINTS
Water Colours These come in small cakes or tubes and they give a transparent finish. They are perfectly alright for dough modelling, however, and I use them if I want to preserve the look of natural salt dough with just a gentle wash of colour. I use water colours mostly on bread dough where it can be blended to get the most delicate and realistic effects, especially on flowers.

17

Acrylic Paints In my opinion, acrylic paints are not suitable for dough modelling. Their natural tendency to dry quickly is accentuated by the porous quality of both salt dough and bread dough. This gives rise to patchiness and makes blending impossible.

Craft Paints These are the little pots of ready-mixed paints for craft workers. Provided that they are water based and non-acrylic, these are fine for dough and are especially good if you do not have the confidence to mix colours.

Poster Paints It is possible to use these on dough, but the results tend to be rather garish and powdery.

Gouache Paints or Designer Colours These are the paints that I use most; so, of course, you would not expect me to say anything but good about them. They come in a range of traditional colours and are perfect for dough modellers. They can be used in an opaque way or watered down and they allow plenty of time for blending.

Brushes The rough surface of salt dough is very hard on brushes, therefore I would advise you mainly to use artists' synthetic brushes. These lose their points very quickly though, so it is useful to buy one or two of the more expensive sable brushes for occasions when a fine point is essential. Sables are also the best brushes to use on bread dough which does not wear them out as quickly as salt dough.

VARNISHES

Salt dough is extremely susceptible to damp and has to be varnished with quite strong varnish to seal it. A good-quality clear, gloss, oil-based polyurethane varnish is best. The sparkle varnishing gives to your work more than compensates for the slight yellowing it may cause.

Do not use a water-based acrylic varnish, even if it does say 'polyurethane' on the tin. Although this does not cause yellowing, being water based it will smudge your painting and ruin it. It is often advisable to use a stronger sealant, such as yacht varnish, on bowls or other pieces that are going to be used and handled a lot. Since this varnish gives an even more yellow finish, use darker colours when painting.

Keep a small soft brush solely for applying varnish and clean it in turpentine or white spirits (mineral spirits), before rinsing it in warm, soapy water.

Bread dough may be varnished with artists' quality, *spirit-based*, acrylic varnish which is clear and quick drying. This varnish is not as strong as polyurethane, but it has the advantage of not yellowing.

Paint Terms and Techniques

Pure This means the colour as it comes from the tube with *just* enough water added to make it flow.

Watery or thin Mix the paint with more water than usual, but stop short of making it transparent.

Transparent Mix the paint with so much water that you are adding just a suggestion of colour to the dough.

Wash A wash is a transparent layer of paint. This sometimes refers to a thin application of paint over a thicker one.

PAINTING FACES

Start the doll's face by painting on some flesh colour and then, while this is still damp, mix a little more Cadmium Red into part of the mixture to get a pink. Work this into the doll's cheeks so that it blends gently into the background colour. If you find this difficult, take a clean damp brush and blend with that. Reserve some of the mixture when you are making the pink, in case you need to return to it for making corrections.

For a standard dough dolly, whose eyes and mouth have been made with a cocktail stick, run a little pale blue around the inside of the eye holes and some mid-pink around the inside of the mouth to complete the face. Sometimes it also looks good to blend a touch of pink onto the fingertips and toes, especially with angels, children and cherubs.

In cases where you have only modelled the nose and have left the eyes and mouth blank, start off in the same way by painting the flesh colour and blending the cheeks, and then continue by painting two very pale blue almonds for the eyes. When dry, encircle the almond shapes with thin black lines and paint in any eyelashes and eyebrows.

Paint a coloured iris in each eye and choose the position and size of them to give expression. Small irises surrounded by white look amazed, whereas large ones painted towards the corners can look quite sultry. When the irises are dry, surround them with a thin black line and paint a small black dot in the middle.

Use a medium pink for the mouth, making it a little browner if your subject is a man and a bright lipstick colour if you are painting that sort of girl. Mouths can add volumes to the personality of the face, but paint the central line between lips with the utmost care as you can make someone look very jolly or utterly miserable, depending on whether the corners turn up or down. Finally, add moustaches, beauty spots or eye shadow.

PAINTING PATTERNS

Paint the base colour and allow to dry.

Spots and dots Use the tip of your brush to paint evenly spaced dots of a similar size all over the base colour. If you are feeling more adventurous, you might like to consider larger spots with golden circles painted around them. These look particularly good on a clown's outfit or a ballet dancer's skirt.

Tartans Use your rigger brush and the main colour to use as a background. When dry, paint some horizontal lines in broad strokes, leaving enough room between the strokes to paint in another line later. Paint similar vertical lines in the same colour.

Then, holding your rigger up on end to produce a thinner stroke, paint a different colour between all the previous lines; horizontally and vertically.

For a more complicated tartan effect, you may also paint a very thin line down the middle of all the broad lines: this works particularly well in black.

FLOWERED PATTERNS

To produce a very simple daisy petal, hold an artist's brush on its point and move it back slowly while allowng more and more of the brush to touch the surface. Complete the stroke by lifting the brush back onto its point and away from the work. Practise this stroke on

Using a rigger brush to paint stripes.

paper first and then, when you have perfected it, make several widely spaced dots over the area that you want to cover and encircle each with a ring of daisy petals. For a variation, put single polka dots among the flowers.

PAINTS USED FOR PROJECTS

Paint	Fruit Bowl	Daffoldil Bowl	Primrose Basket	Strawberry Basket	Mother's Day Dish	Victorian Wreath	Fruit Garland	Flower Garland	Fruit Wreath	Christmas Wreath	Thanksgiving Wreath	Victorian Girl	George	Catherine Sheep	Heathcliff Pig	Finley Fish	Claude	Mr Bear Portrait	Mrs Bear Portrait	Halloween Witch	Nanny and Baby Rabbit
Lemon Yellow		●	●					●		●											
Cadmium Yellow										●	●	●	●							●	
Golden Yellow	●	●			●	●	●	●	●												
Yellow Ochre																		●	●		
Ultramarine				●	●			●		●		●	●	●		●	●				●
Olive Green	●		●	●	●	●	●	●	●												
Fir Green										●											
Viridian																●				●	
Saffron Green																					
Sap Green		●															●				
Linden Green	●						●		●												
Permanent Green Middle																		●	●		
Rose Madder		●	●		●																
Cadmium Red										●	●	●	●							●	
Rose Malmaison	●					●	●	●	●												
Rose Pink																					
Alizarin Crimson												●		●	●			●		●	●
Red Ochre				●								●	●					●	●		
Spectrum Red	●				●		●		●	●											
Flame Red																					
Magenta																●				●	
Spectrum Violet	●					●	●	●	●			●								●	
Burnt Sienna																					
Raw Umber		●								●		●	●					●	●	●	●
Lamp Black					●		●					●	●	●	●	●	●	●			
Jet Black											●									●	●
Permanent White	●		●	●	●	●	●	●	●	●		●	●	●		●	●	●	●	●	●
Silver																●					
Gold					●	●				●								●	●	●	

20

Bridal Couple	Mother and Baby with pram	Carol Singers	Nursery Window	Cat Napping	Rose Cottage	House with Georgian Door	Town House	Kitchen Dresser	Twisted Floral Initial	Clown Initial	Initial with Figure	Ballet Dancer Initial	Tennis Player Initial	Christmas Labels	Father Christmas	Christmas Teddies	Winged Head Cherub	Garlanded Cherub	Rocking Horse	Christmas Stockings
●									●			●	●	●						
●	●	●		●	●		●	●	●	●		●			●					●
								●												
		●	●		●			●												●
	●			●		●		●				●			●		●	●		
●	●	●	●		●	●	●	●				●	●	●				●		
		●																	●	●
						●														
																				●
				●																
					●												●	●		
●	●	●				●	●			●	●	●	●		●					●
								●	●											
																				●
●				●			●													
	●		●	●	●	●		●			●									
				●											●	●	●		●	
						●													●	●
		●	●			●				●										
		●	●			●	●						●							
		●				●	●						●	●	●					
		●	●		●		●			●					●	●	●			
●	●	●				●	●						●						●	●
●	●	●	●	●	●	●	●	●	●	●	●	●	●	●	●	●	●	●	●	●
	●												●		●					
●		●	●				●			●			●			●	●	●		

Colour	Gingerbread Men and Women	Christmas Tree Angel	Nativity Scene	Easter Centrepiece	Candelabra	Christmas Place Names	Christmas Napkin Rings	Festive Table Centrepiece	Thanksgiving Sheaf	Love Birds Heart	Entwined Hearts	Valentine's Day Mirror	Cherubs and Hearts	Engagement Bowl	Tree Decorations and Tags:	Walkings Sticks, page 105	Christmas Tree, page 100	Christmas Puddings, page 97
Lemon Yellow				●				●				●	●	●				
Cadmium Yellow		●	●															
Golden Yellow				●						●								
Yellow Ochre			●															
Ultramarine	●	●	●	●						●	●	●	●	●			●	●
Olive Green				●		●	●	●		●	●	●	●	●		●	●	
Fir Green																		●
Viridian	●					●												
Saffron Green																	●	
Sap Green																		
Linden Green								●										
Permanent Green Middle																		
Rose Madder				●							●	●		●				
Cadmium Red	●	●	●					●										
Rose Malmaison																		
Rose Pink												●					●	
Alizarin Crimson		●							●	●								
Red Ochre	●		●															
Spectrum Red						●	●									●		
Flame Red																		●
Magenta																		
Spectrum Violet				●													●	
Burnt Sienna			●															●
Raw Umber																	●	
Lamp Black																		
Jet Black	●		●					●	●									●
Permanent White	●	●	●	●	●					●	●	●	●	●			●	●
Silver																		
Gold		●	●							●	●	●	●				●	●

THE CRACKING PROBLEM

- Cracking is the bane of a dough modeller's life and even though there does not seem to be a clear-cut solution, there are some tips which might help. Do not model with dough that is too soft, because it has a tendency to dent and cracks form along the dents as it dries. Soft dough can be caused by too much water or by too little salt.
- Make sure that you knead your dough thoroughly so that no air remains; trapped air expands in the oven and it then cracks the dough.
- If the dough is too dry, it will actually be covered in minute cracks before baking, and these will inevitably expand in the heat.
- I have added *a little* oil to the basic dough mixture to help alleviate the problem of cracking, but do not be tempted to add more oil as the dough will then take hours longer to bake and end up stuck to the baking tray. You will then probably still crack it, trying to prise it off!
- Cook dough at as low a temperature, and for as long as, possible; in fact, you should think of the process as 'drying' rather than 'cooking'. I have given good average times and settings for drying the dough, but if you are willing to experiment with your oven, you may find that leaving the dough in for a much longer time at a lower setting will avoid the problem of cracking.
- Leave the dough in the oven to cool down slowly after it has cooked and you have turned off the heat.
- To repair a crack quickly, fill it with a hard-drying glue and use reasonably thick paint to cover the glue. Alternatively, fill it with soft dough, then smooth it over and bake it again. Rub it down with fine sandpaper before painting. You may also use fine surface filler and follow the instructions on the packet.

OTHER PROBLEMS

Rope splits vertically

- Dough not kneaded properly. Scoop up dough, re-knead and start again.

Discoloured and dented model

- Too liberal use of water when fixing pieces together. Dampen the piece being attached rather than the main model.
- Denting caused by dough being too soft.

Blisters on flat model

- Insufficient kneading or too high oven temperature. Check dough after 20 minutes and prick blisters, weigh down and bake.

Baked item will not leave baking sheet. Usually happens to dense models

- Dough not cooked. Run a palette knife under it to release and pierce dough with fine needle from the back: if it goes in easily and comes out smeared, dough is not cooked. Turn model upside down on foil and continue baking until hard.

Model drops off the wall, leaving a rusty hook

- Dough hanging in damp atmosphere or on damp wall softens.

BASKETS AND BOWLS

B owls are among my favourite projects because they have everything: they are easy to make, look impressive as gifts, and are versatile and useful as well.

The basic technique of weaving dough, either on the inside or the outside of an ovenproof dish, is very simple; however, it is important to choose the dish with care. If you are modelling on the outside of the dish, make sure that it does not have a rim under which the dough can get caught as it expands slightly during baking. On the other hand, if you are weaving dough on the inside of the dish, you will need a rim to support the decoration.

Decorating the dish is the best stage of the modelling. Although I have used flowers and fruit in this book, you might like to experiment with other designs, such as different-shaped breads, shells and fish. Alternatively, you may prefer to concentrate on one type of fruit, such as cherries or strawberries, on any one project.

A basket, such as the Primrose Basket, see page 28, is the first item I demonstrate to beginners because it includes almost all the basic techniques of dough modelling. By the time you have woven and twisted the basket, then made the leaves and flowers you will almost be a fully fledged dough modeller.

Fruit Bowl
Weaving strips of dough over an ovenproof bowl.

·FRUIT BOWL·

ovenproof bowl, see method
cooking oil
¾ quantity Paste Dough, see page 10
Egg Glaze, see page 11
leaf cutters: ivy, rose and a very small cutter
black stamens
cloves
primrose cutter

1 You need an ovenproof bowl without a lip or rim. My bowl measured 16.5cm (6½in) in diameter and 10cm (4in) deep but the size may vary slightly according to what is available. Brush the outside of the bowl with oil and invert it on a baking sheet.
2 Using half the dough, make a twist to encircle the now-inverted top of the bowl, see page 12. Arrange this on the sheet, around the bowl and fix the individual ropes of dough together with a little water to avoid having an obvious join in the twist.
3 Roll out the remaining dough to 6mm (¼ in) thick and cut ten strips approximately 25 × 2.5cm (10 × 1in) depending upon the exact size of your bowl. Weave the strips over the bowl, see page 12, and leave their ends overhanging the twist on the baking sheet.
4 When the weaving is complete, trim each strip, brush the end with a little water and fix it to the twist. Brush with glaze, then bake at 145°C (290°F/Gas 1½) for about 1 hour. Leave to cool on the baking sheet.
5 Remove the bowl from the mould and stand it the right way up. Knead the scraps

Fruit Bowl

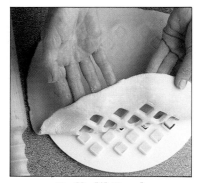

Daffodil Bowl

Using a lattice pie top cutter to make the bowl.

and trimmings of dough from making the bowl and divide this in half. Reserve one piece for modelling the fruit and roll out the rest thinly.

6 Cut out eight rose leaves and vein them with the back of a knife. Arrange these in pairs at regular intervals around the rim of the bowl, fixing them in place with a little water.

7 Mould eight small balls from the remaining dough to represent cherries. Cut the thick ends from the stamens and push one into each cherry. Push the rest of the stamens into the opposite side of the cherries to represent stalks. Arrange the cherries in pairs, close to the leaves. Tuck the loose ends of the stamens under the leaves.

8 Mould two or three slightly larger balls of dough into apples and arrange them around the dish. Use the very small leaf cutter to make a leaf for each apple and attach this to the top, with a clove for a stalk.

9 Model similar pieces of dough into pears and place them randomly between the other fruit. Press a clove right into the dough at the base of each pear, leaving just the star-shaped end showing. Push another clove into the top to resemble the stalk.

10 Build up a bunch of grapes on each side of the rim using very small balls of dough. Cut out an ivy leaf and place this at the broad end of the bunch, with a stalk made from a clove.

11 Cut out some primroses and a few leaves to fill in any spaces. Stand the bowl on the baking sheet. Brush the inside with glaze, taking care not to get any glaze on the fruit, leaves or flowers. Bake at 145°C (290°F/Gas 1 ½) for 1 hour.

Painting and Finishing

● Paint the leaves and fruit as for the Fruit Garland, see page 36. Varnish several times, inside and out, with yacht varnish.

·DAFFODIL BOWL·

¾ *quantity Paste Dough, see page 10*
lattice pastry cutter
cooking oil
ovenproof dish with lip
daffodil cutters
cocktail stick (toothpick)

1 Roll out half the dough on a lightly floured board until large enough to cover the lattice pie cutter and about 6mm (¼ in) thick.

2 Place the cutter on the board, cutting edge up, and lay the rolled-out dough over it. Roll over the dough lightly until you can see that the lattice has been cut.

3 Oil the dish and line it with the dough lattice, making sure that the lattice pattern is symmetrical. Trim off excess dough draped over the outer edge of the rim.

4 Use half the remaining dough to make a rope long enough to encircle the top of the pie dish, see page 11. Dampen the lattice rim and fix the rope on top, flattening it with your fingers until it is the same width as the lip, starting and finishing at one corner.

5 Roll four fine ropes of dough to represent daffodil stems and fix one of these on each side of the rim. Roll four similar stems each with one end slightly fatter. Model the thick ends into daffodil buds. Fix these in place alongside the first stems.

6 Roll out the rest of the dough. Make four daffodils, see page 17, then arrange them on the plain stems. Cut out eight narrow, pointed leaves, see page 15, and arrange these beside the daffodils, two to each flower. Model a little bird, see page 15, and place him somewhere on the rim among the flowers to complete the decoration. Bake at 145°C (290°F/Gas 1½) for 2 hours.

Daffodil Bowl

Painting and Finishing

● Paint the leaves and stems with a thin mixture of Sap Green. While the bud stalk is still damp, blend a little watery Raw Umber into the bud base before painting most of the rest of the bud in Sap Green, just leaving a 'V' shaped opening at the top for the tip of the flower. Leave to dry.

Paint the petals and the tips of the buds Lemon Yellow. Allow to dry before painting the trumpets Golden Yellow, tipped while still damp with a mixture of Golden Yellow and Rose Madder. Paint the bird Lemon Yellow, then blend some of the Golden Yellow and Rose Madder mix on his chest and wing tips. Varnish inside and out with two or three coats of yacht varnish.

·PRIMROSE BASKET·

1 quantity Basic Dough, see page 10
fresh primrose leaf
primrose cutter
modelling tool

1 Roll out half the dough to 6mm ($\frac{1}{4}$in) thick, then cut it into nine 15cm × 12mm (6 × $\frac{1}{2}$in) strips. Working directly on a baking sheet, weave a mat which is four strips high and five strips wide, see page 12. Trim the strips so that the ends of each lay touching the baking sheet.

2 Roll two 15cm (6in) long finger-thick ropes from some of the remaining dough. Lay these vertically along either edge of the woven piece, flatten them, then trim off any excess.

3 Make a twist from two similar ropes, see page 12, and lay this across the bottom of the basket, then trim it to size. Make a 25cm (10in) twist and attach it to either side of the top of the basket to form a handle.

4 Make a third twist, about 20cm (8in) long, and fix this horizontally across the top of the basket, curving it down slightly in the middle so that the lattice shows above it. This twist should conceal the handle joins.

5 Knead all the remaining dough together and roll it out thinly. Cut out about five primrose leaves using the fresh leaves as a guide and to imprint the vein pattern on the dough, see page 16. Arrange these on the basket so that some of them drape over the edge and a couple stand at the back attached to the lattice.

6 Cut out at least 20 primroses and arrange them on the basket. The flowers should overlap each other in some places. Indent the middle of each flower with a modelling tool. Bake at 145°C (290°F/Gas 1$\frac{1}{2}$) for about 2$\frac{1}{2}$ hours.

Painting and Finishing

● Make a soft watery green by mixing Lemon Yellow and a little white into Olive Green. Paint the primrose leaves with this, making sure that the paint is thin so that the veins show up well. Mix a little white and Lemon Yellow together and paint the flowers. Use the mixed green to paint their centres while the yellow is still fairly damp.

Make an orange colour by adding a little Rose Madder to the Lemon Yellow and use to encircle the green centres when they are quite dry. Varnish once or twice with polyurethane clear gloss varnish.

CRAFT TIP

If you want to make a flower bud, stamp out the primrose flower, then fold it into quarters and set the pointed end into a small oval of dough. Attach a dough stalk.

Primrose Basket

Strawberry Basket

Pressing a lump of dough against a basket to leave the impression of the weave on the dough.

·STRAWBERRY BASKET·

1 quantity Basic Dough, see page 10
basket or woven cane object
leaf cutter
cocktail stick (toothpick)
calyx cutter
small primrose cutter
modelling tool
Egg Glaze, see page 11

1   Form a good handful of dough into a ball, then press it firmly against a basket or some other cane object so that the pattern of the weave is imprinted on the dough.

2   Carefully mould the dough into a basket shape without pressing out the impression of the weave. Place it on a baking sheet. Cut a shallow curve out of the dough to form the top of the basket. Make a twist of dough, approximately 12.5cm (5in) long, see page 12, to trim the top edge.

3   Make a slightly thicker, 22.5cm (9in) long twist of dough and fix this in place on either side of the curve in the dough to make a handle. Place a third, thinner 17.5cm (7in) twist across the middle of the basket for decoration. Lastly, make a thin 4cm (1½in) rope and fix it around the bottom of the basket as a base.

4   Roll out half the remaining dough thinly and cut out nine leaves. Vein these with the back of a knife and arrange them in the basket so that some of them are draped over the front of it and over the joins between the handle and basket. Position a few leaves at the back of the basket but do not fix them to the dough until the strawberries are added.

5   Divide the remaining dough in half. Using one portion of the dough, model nine strawberries about the size of small, real fruit. Use a cocktail stick (toothpick) to mark a strawberry-like texture on the moulded fruit.

6   Roll out the second portion of dough, then use the calyx cutter to stamp out a top for each strawberry and fix to the top of each fruit before arranging the strawberries in the basket. Make sure that some of them are attached to the loose leaves at the back of the basket. Secure the leaves when the fruit are in position.

7   Cut out several small primroses. Arrange them around the strawberries and place a tiny ball of dough in the centre of each, then indent it with a modelling tool.

8   Brush the basket with Egg Glaze, avoiding the parts to be painted and the twists on the basket itself. Bake at 145°C (290°F/Gas 1½) for 2½ hours.

Painting and Finishing

● Paint all the leaves and strawberry tops with Olive Green and the strawberries with Spectrum Red. Mix a little Red Ochre into some Permanent White to make the dusky pink for the flowers, then when they are dry paint their centres with Golden Yellow. Encircle the centres with a mixture of Olive Green and Permanent White. Varnish with polyurethane clear gloss varnish.

Strawberry Basket

Mother's Day Dish
*Adding the strip around the rim —
the excess length is coiled and butted
up to the first corner of
the dish.*

*Attaching the top strip with second
pair of coils and adding the
decorative marks.*

·MOTHER'S DAY DISH·

ovenproof dish with lip, see method
¾ quantity Paste Dough, see page 10
cooking oil
old retractable ballpoint pen
rose cutters • leaf cutters
blossom plunger cutter

1   You may use an ovenproof dish of any size providing that it has a rim. I used a dish measuring 24 × 17.5 × 5cm (9½ × 7 × 2in). Brush the inside and rim of the dish with oil and place it on a baking sheet.

2   Roll out two-thirds of the dough to 6mm (¼ in) thick, then cut out nine 30 × 2cm (12 × ¾ in) strips. Weave the dough strips into a lattice, inside the dish, see page 12, making sure that each strip overlaps the rim lip. Trim the strips to the edge of the dish.

3   Knead any excess dough with trimmings and roll out into a long narrow shape so that you can cut several 2cm (¾ in) wide strips. Coil the first 6.5cm (2½ in) of one strip and place it on one corner of the dish. Fix the rest of the strip over the woven dough ends around the rim. Add further strips, making neat joins in the dough to cover the weaving all around the rim and to allow a 6.5cm (2½ in) length of dough spare. Coil the excess dough in the opposite direction to the first piece, then fix it back-to-back with the existing coil. Repeat once more, making slightly shorter coils of 4cm (1½ in) and butting them up to the first coils. Use the old pen to mark a pattern of dots all around the dough rim.

4   Make one large and two small roses, see page 15. Arrange the roses on the corner opposite the coils, with the largest rose in the middle. Cut out four medium leaves, mark veins on them, then arrange them in pairs on either side of the roses. Place a group of three small blossoms close to the roses on each set of leaves. Bake at 145°C (290°F/Gas 1½) for about 1½ hours.

Painting and Finishing

●   Add very little Ultramarine to Permanent White for very pale blue. Using this very thinly, paint the rim of the dish.

Paint patchy, watery Olive Green on the leaves so that some of the dough is uncovered. While still wet, paint thin Rose Madder on the patches and blend with a clean damp brush. Paint the roses and the dots on the lip with Permanent White. While the roses are damp, tip their petal edges with Rose Madder. Blend this towards the centre of each petal with a clean damp brush. Use the pale blue to paint the blossoms and blush with a little Rose Madder. Line both layers of the edge with Gold and continue the lines around the coils on the inside and outside. Encircle each white dot with gold. Varnish inside and outside with two or three coats of yacht varnish.

Mother's Day Dish

GARLANDS AND WREATHS

Victorian Wreath
Indenting the centres of the flowers as the decoration is built up on the wreath.

In the following designs, I have tried to avoid the rather folksy tradition related to making garlands and wreaths. There is no reason why dough should be limited to rustic subjects, as it so often is, and you will find that it is possible to borrow ideas from a far wider range of artistic traditions and to translate them successfully into dough-modelling techniques. The flower garland on page 38, for example, was inspired by the border on an old porcelain plate, while the fruit garland owes its existence to a Victorian frieze.

Look for inspiration in medieval wood carvings or sculpture, as well as paintings, illustrations, textile designs and so on. You never know — you might move dough modelling out of the kitchen and into the drawing room.

· VICTORIAN WREATH ·

25cm (10in) round plate
1¼ quantities Basic Dough, see page 10
large leaf cutter
rose cutters
modelling tool
blossom plunger cutter

1 Using a dinner plate as a template, draw a circle on a baking sheet using a pencil or felt-tip pen.
2 Use slightly more than half the dough to make a rope measuring 75cm (30in) long. Arrange this just inside the circle on the baking tray and join the ends of the dough with a little water to make a ring. Keep the

join at the base of your design. Flatten the rope slightly with your fingers so that it is about 5cm (2in) wide.
3 Roll out approximately two-thirds of the remaining dough and cut out 29 leaves. Use the back of a knife to make veins on the leaves and arrange them on the wreath. Fix four leaves pointing right, four pointing left and one pointing straight down over the join in the wreath. Halfway up on either side of the wreath, fix eight leaves: four pointing up and four pointing down. Set aside the remaining four leaves.
4 Make three roses, see page 15, and place one in the centre of each group of leaves. Make six small roses, omitting the final four petals, and arrange these in pairs on either side of the large roses.
5 Model a large bow, see page 13, extending the ribbons to about 17.5cm (7in). Arrange this at the top of the wreath, curling the ribbons with their ends tucked behind the groups of roses.
6 Arrange the reserved leaves in pairs in the curves of ribbon on either side of the bow. Make two small roses and place on the leaves.
7 Model two little birds, see page 15, and place them facing one another on either side of the base group of roses.
8 To make the sprays of flowers between the birds and roses, roll out four fine ropes, approximately 4cm (1½in) long. Arrange these in pairs to represent stalks, with the ends nearest the roses joined together. Using a sharp knife, cut four elongated leaves from rolled-out dough and arrange them in pairs at

Victorian Wreath

the base of the stalks. To make the flowers, build up several little balls of dough at the tops of the stalks and indent each one with a modelling tool.

9 Cut out about 30 small blossoms and arrange these liberally all over the wreath wherever there is a bare space. Indent the centres of the blossoms with a modelling tool.

10 Use a modelling tool to make two holes behind the bow at the top of the wreath to hang it when finished. Bake at 145°C (290°F/ Gas 1½) for about 3 hours.

Painting and Finishing

● Paint the leaves with patchy, watery Olive Green, leaving occasional uneven patches bare. While still damp, wash some thin Rose Malmaison on the bare patches and blend with a clean damp brush.

Paint the roses individually with thin Permanent White and tip the edges of the petals with some Rose Malmaison while still damp. Gently blend the colour down into the petals with a clean damp brush.

Paint the little birds white. Blend a little Rose Malmaison into their chests and some thin Ultramarine on the tips of their tails and wings.

Mix some Permanent White with some Ultramarine and paint the little blossoms like forget-me-knots, blushing the blue slightly with a little thin Rose Malmaison. Paint the small sprays of flowers white. Mix a little Olive Green into white to paint the leaves and stalks. Dab a little of this pale green into the centre of each flower.

Mix some Spectrum Violet with an equal amount of Permanent White to paint the bow and edge it with Gold when dry. Finally, paint the centres of the forget-me-knots and the birds' beaks with Golden Yellow. When dry, varnish with clear gloss polyurethane varnish.

CRAFT TIP

Holes in garlands are for hanging; hooks are for tying decorative ribbons through.

·FRUIT GARLAND·

1 quantity Basic Dough, see page 10
leaf cutters
cloves
50cm (20in) net
butterfly cutter
small primrose cutter
modelling tool
Hanging Hooks, see page 17

1 Take some dough and make two ropes, see page 12, each 30cm (12in) long and tapered slightly at both ends. Wind the ropes together into a twist, see page 12, and curve this slightly as you place it on a baking sheet.

2 Roll out a small piece of dough, then cut out several leaves of various sizes and mark veins on them using the back of a knife. Arrange these at random on the garland, saving a few to fill any spaces later.

3 Make two or three balls of dough for apples and fix them on the garland among the leaves. Push a clove into each apple, star-shaped end first, so that the stalk is left sticking out.

4 Model two or three similar balls, only this time taper one end of each slightly to make a pear shape. Arrange on the garland. Push a clove, stalk end first, into the broad end of each pear. Discard the stars from two or three cloves and push the stalks, cut ends first, into the tops of the pears.

5 Working directly on the garland, build up tiny balls of dough into two or three bunches of grapes. Finish these by adding a clove stalk at the broadest end of each bunch.

6 Cut several pieces of net, each approximately 5cm (2in) square. Place a small ball of dough in the centre of a square of net. Gather up the net around the dough, then squeeze the dough out through the holes. As the dough is

Fruit Garland and Flower Garland, see page 38

Fruit Garland

Squeezing the dough through a small piece of net to make a blackberry.

Carefully use a knife to transfer the blackberry from the net directly to the garland.

CRAFT TIP

The holes in the garland allow nails to be used to secure it safely to a wall.

---

forced through the net it forms a blackberry-shaped ball: remove this carefully by sliding a knife underneath it and transfer it straight to the twist. Fix the blackberries in groups of three or four, securing them with a little water.

7 Mould several balls the size of small cherries and arrange them in pairs on the twist. Roll very thin ropes of dough for the stalks and arrange these on the cherries, joining the stalk ends of each pair together.

8 Model fairly small oval shapes for plums and mark a groove down each with the back of a knife. Arrange these in groups of three.

9 Roll out some dough and cut out a butterfly, see page 14, then arrange it on the garland. Stamp out small primroses and use them, with the reserved leaves, to fill gaps on the garland. Make sure that you leave a little of the dough showing through, otherwise the decoration will look a little cluttered.

10 Use a modelling tool to make a hole 6mm ($\frac{1}{4}$ in) from the edge of the dough at each end of the garland. Push two hanging hooks into the ends, then bake the garland at 145°C (290°F/Gas 1$\frac{1}{2}$) for about 2$\frac{1}{2}$ hours.

Painting and Finishing

● Paint the apples with watery Linden Green, then while still damp streak them gently with equally watery Spectrum Red. Do not add red all over but keep it more or less on one side and around the stalk. Blend these colours together with a clean damp brush. Treat the pears in the same way using Golden Yellow instead of Linden Green.

Paint the grapes in pure Spectrum Violet and add a little Rose Malmaison to this to paint the plums. Add a little more Rose Malmaison to get a purple-red which is just right for painting the cherries.

Paint the blackberries with a brushful of clear water before adding some thin Lamp Black. Leave a small irregular patch of the blackberry unpainted and trickle some watery Linden Green and Rose Malmaison on this patch, so that the paint merges with the black and gives the appearance of under-ripe fruit. Paint the leaves in a similar way, using Olive Green as the base coat, and Rose Malmaison and Golden Yellow for the patches. Blend these colours with a clean damp brush.

Paint the flowers a dull dusty pink by mixing a little white into the cherry mixture. When they are quite dry, add a centre of Golden Yellow tipped with a little purple. Finish by painting the cherry stalks with Lamp Black and the butterfly in warm oranges and yellows, made by mixing Rose Malmaison and Golden Yellow. When dry, varnish with clear gloss polyurethane varnish.

·*FLOWER GARLAND*·

$\frac{3}{4}$ quantity Basic Dough, see page 10
leaf cutters
rose cutters
carnation cutters
daffodil cutters
primrose cutters
blossom plunger cutter
wooden skewer
butterfly cutter
black stamens
Hanging Hooks, see page 17

1 Roll half the dough into a rope, see page 11, approximately 15cm (6in) long. Leave the middle section of the dough, then extend and taper both ends until the rope measures about 30cm (12in). Avoid making the tapered ends too thin by reducing the length slightly if necessary. Curve the rope on a baking sheet and flatten it slightly with your fingers.

2 Roll out some dough, then cut out several leaves in various sizes and use the back of a knife to mark veins on them. Arrange the leaves in pairs at both ends of the curved dough: four leaves on either side is usually enough, with the smallest ones nearer the end, all facing the middle. Arrange four large leaves in the middle, so that they cover the base and point outwards. There should be room for another two pairs of leaves, halfway between the middle set and the leaves placed at the ends of the garland.

3 Make a rose, see page 15, and a carnation, see page 16, and arrange them back to back on the centre group of leaves. Make two smaller roses without the final four petals and tuck them into the sets of end leaves. Make two daffodils, see page 17, and place these on the midway pair of leaves.

4 Make two violets, see page 16, and tuck them into the centre arrangement with the rose and carnation. Cut out several large and small primroses, and small blossoms, then use to fill spaces on the garland. Place a small ball of dough in the centre of each of the larger primroses, then use a skewer to indent this and the centres of the other small flowers.

5 Cut out a butterfly, see page 14, for the top of the garland. Trim two of the black stamens and push them into one end of the butterfly's body to represent antennae. Prop up the wings with small rolls of foil if necessary.

6 Use a skewer to make a hole 6mm ($\frac{1}{4}$ in) from the edge of the dough at either end of the garland. Fix two hanging hooks at the extreme ends and bake at 145°C (290°F/Gas $1\frac{1}{2}$) for $2\frac{1}{2}$ hours.

Painting and Finishing

● Paint patchy watery Olive Green on the leaves so that some of the dough is uncovered. While still wet add a touch of Rose Malmaison and blend lightly with a clean damp brush.

Paint the roses with pure Rose Malmaison and add a little Spectrum Violet to the mixture to paint the larger primrose-shaped flowers. Paint the outer petals of the daffodils with pure Lemon Yellow and add a little Permanent White to this mixture to paint the smaller primroses. The trumpets of the daffodils and the centres of the larger primroses are painted with Golden Yellow and edged with a mixture of Golden Yellow and Rose Malmaison.

Paint the carnation with Permanent White and, while still damp, tip the edges with some watery Rose Malmaison so that it bleeds into the white a little. Paint the blossoms with a mixture of Ultramarine and Permanent White, then just touch them with pink so that they resemble forget-me-knots. The violets are painted with pure Spectrum Violet and their stamens painted in pale yellow.

The small primroses have Olive Green centres bordered with Golden Yellow. The butterfly can be any combination of colours, you choose; however, this one is mainly painted with a mixture of Golden Yellow and Rose Malmaison on the wings, tipped with Ultramarine and white. When dry, varnish with clear gloss polyurethane varnish.

CRAFT TIP

The Flower Garland has a list of equipment which looks impressive and expensive but, although helpful, is not essential. The very small blossoms are difficult to make without cutters but they can be replaced by little flowers made from very small balls of dough, fixed in place, then indented with the end of a modelling tool. All the remaining decoration can be made using a sharp knife, a pair of curved nail scissors and a wooden skewer.

Join the ends with water, smooth with a modelling tool, then flatten the ring with your fingers to about 4.5cm (1¾ in) wide. Make two holes through the dough, opposite the join, for threading ribbon to hang the wreath.

2 Roll out half the remaining dough thinly and cut out 24 large leaves. Mark veins in these and arrange randomly on the ring often overlapping the edge, leaving room for fruit.

3 Following the instructions on page 36, make five apples and five pears and arrange these in pairs evenly around the wreath. Make two pairs of cherries and place these on either side, adding a couple of small leaves to cover the ends of the stalks. Model two or three sets of blackberries and plums and arrange these to balance your design.

4 Arrange a bunch of grapes, see page 36, and a small group of strawberries, see page 30, towards the bottom of the wreath.

5 Finally, cut out a few small flowers and fix them here and there where you think they are necessary. Indent the flower centres with a modelling tool and bake at 145°C (290°F/ Gas 1½) for 3 hours.

Painting and Finishing

● Paint patchy, watery Olive Green on the leaves so that some dough is uncovered. While still wet, paint thin Rose Malmaison over the patches and blend the colours with a clean dry brush.

When the leaves are dry, paint the fruit, see page 38 – first the apples and pears; dry before attempting the plums and grapes. Then paint the cherries and the strawberries, see page 30. Paint the flowers first with Permanent White, then add a little watery Rose Malmaison, before they are quite dry. Blend the colour a little with a clean, dry brush. Finish by

Fruit Wreath

CRAFT TIP

To make hanging holes, simply wobble the end of a sharp modelling tool through the dough until the hole is large enough. Alternatively a far neater hole is made by using a plastic drinking straw to remove a little plug of dough.

·FRUIT WREATH·

10cm (4in) round saucer
1¼ quantities Basic Dough, see page 10
modelling tool
large and very small leaf cutters
cloves • small piece of net
calyx cutter
cocktail stick (toothpick)
blossom plunger cutter

1 Using the saucer, draw a circle on a baking sheet. Roll half the dough into a 35cm (14in) rope. Form the rope into a ring on the circle.

painting the blackberries. Varnish with one or two coats of clear gloss polyurethane varnish and add a ribbon bow.

· CHRISTMAS WREATH ·

1¼ quantities Basic Dough, see page 10
25cm (10in) plate
large holly leaf cutter
primrose cutter · stamens
large and small leaf cutters
cocktail stick (toothpick)
large plastic drinking straw
Hanging Hook, see page 17
1m (40in) red ribbon

1   Lay the plate on a baking tray and draw around it with a pencil. If the tray is very dark you may need to use a coloured pencil. Make a thick rope from half the dough, long enough to encircle the plate – about 70cm (28in). Lay the rope on the mark and join the ends by trimming each at an opposite slant and fixing them with water. Press the ring flat with your fingers until it is about 4cm (1½in) wide.

2   Make the arms and legs for the cherub, see page 13. Lay them at the top of the ring so that the finished cherub will cover the join, but do not secure the left hand. Model a generous pear shape for the body and lay this on the arms and legs. Separate the buttocks by making a line with the back of your knife.

3   Make a head with a smiling face, see page 134, and fix this facing forwards and resting on the left arm. Roll out some dough to 3mm (⅛in) thick and cut out two large leaves. Lay these together on the board and notch the outside edges of both to make a pair of wings. Fix the wings onto the cherub's back with the notched edge uppermost.

4   Make five pencil-thin ropes about 15cm (6in) long and drape these over and around the wreath so that they appear to be one continuous rope wound around it. Start the first one on the inside, just under the cherub's legs, and lay it diagonally across the wreath so that it finishes on the outside. Trim the ends of all the ropes at a slant so that they fit neatly against the sides of the wreath. Start the second rope on the inside and not quite opposite the first one and lay this across the wreath in the same way. Continue around the wreath in this fashion until the last rope ends close to the cherub's right hand.

5   Cut out 30 to 35 holly leaves and arrange these in groups of four or five on each of the ropes. Arrange similar groups between these, directly on the wreath, leaving a space of about 7.5cm (3in) at the bottom of the wreath. Make several holly berries from balls of dough and put three or four in the centre of each group of leaves. Place one berry in the left hand of the cherub, as if he is picking them.

6   Make a robin, see page 15, and sit him on the wreath close to, and facing, the cherub. Cut out about 10 primroses and flatten their petals slightly, see page 16. Keeping the space at the bottom, place flowers symmetrically around the wreath. Push three shortened stamens into the centre of each.

7   Finally, use the drinking sraw to make two holes, 5cm (2in) apart, in the space and push a hanging hook into the top behind the cherub. Bake at 145°C (290°F/Gas 1½) for 2½ hours.

Painting and Finishing

●   Mix up some flesh colour and paint all the cherub apart from his wings and hair. While still wet, mix a spot of Cadmium Red with watery white and blend this into his cheeks, fingers and toes, running a little into the line of his mouth. Paint his wings white and then add a touch of Ultramarine to make a pale

CRAFT TIP

Traditionally, holly wreaths are meant to be hung on the front door as a sign of welcome but unless you live in particularly sunny climes I would hang this dough wreath inside the house or it is likely to soften.

*Draping a pencil-thin rope around
the wreath.*

FLESH COLOUR

To make flesh colour you
need Permanent White,
Cadmium Yellow and
Cadmium Red. Take the
white first and add a little
water, then add a small
amount of yellow and mix
it in well. Follow this with
a very small amount of the
red and mix it in well. If
the mixture looks too
orange, add more white. The
result should be a pale peach
colour and definitely not
pink or orange.

blue. Blend this colour into the ends of his
wings and also use it to paint his eyes. When
his wings are quite dry, tip their very ends with
Gold and use the same colour to paint his hair.

Add a little Fir Green to watery Burnt
Umber to paint the holly branch and leave to
dry. Paint each bunch of leaves separately
using pure Fir Green, with Lemon Yellow
blended along the edges of each leaf. Use pure
Spectrum Red to paint the berries.

Paint the flowers white and work on only
two or three at a time to blend a mixture of
Lemon Yellow and a touch of Fir Green into
their centres and onto their stamens before the
white dries. Mix a little Raw Umber into some
white to paint the robin's head, back and
wings. When this is dry, paint his chest and
under his chin with Spectrum Red. Take some
fairly fluid Raw Umber onto a fine brush and
paint a stylized feather pattern on his back, tail
and wings; add a dot of the same colour to his
eyes. I have also decorated his feathers with
little dots of Gold. Varnish the wreath. When
dry, thread some wide red ribbon through the
holes in the bottom and tie a bow.

THANKSGIVING · WREATH ·

1½ quantities Basic Dough, see page 10
25cm (10in) plate
15cm (6in) saucer · nail scissors
fine floristry wire
cocktail stick (toothpick)
large plastic drinking straw
wide strip cutter
Egg Glaze, see page 11
Hanging Hook, see page 17
2m (2¼yd) ribbon · Blu-Tack
small bunch of dried flowers (optional)

1   Roll out a third of the dough to 6mm (¼in)
thick. Using the larger plate as a template, cut
out a circle of dough and place it on a baking
tray. Position the saucer in the middle of the
circle and use that as a template to cut out the
centre.

2   Gather up any scraps of dough and knead
them back into the main ball of dough. Roll
eight thin 10cm (4in) long ropes of dough and
lay them side by side and diagonally over the
bottom of the dough ring. Tuck the ends under
the ring and secure them in place with a little
water.

3   Make seven similar ropes and model ears
of corn. Trim two to 17.5cm (7in) and 15cm
(6in), and five to 12.5cm (5in). Take the
longest one first and arrange it at a slant, so
that the stalk lies over the first group of ropes,
slanting in the opposite direction and about
one third of the way along from the inside
edge. Tuck the stalk under the inside of the
ring and allow the head to lay on the baking
tray. Arrange the 15cm (6in) stalk in a
similar manner, laying it close to the first.
Arrange two of the remaining stalks on either
side and secure the last three on top, with two

Christmas Wreath

Laying the ears of corn on the wreath.

Putting on the second set of ropes.

of them curving outwards. When you have finished this arrangement there should still be at least half of the first group of ropes showing.

4 Roll a second set of eight ropes and lay these in a similar way to the first set, working on the opposite slant and starting off by covering the exposed corner of the original ropes. Make a further set of ropes, this time making the eighth one complete with an ear of wheat. Lay these in place diagonally, in the opposite direction to the previous set and so that they cover the foremost corner of it.

5 Work your way around the ring adding ropes of dough in this manner, always changing direction with each set and always covering the corner of the previous set. Work a head of corn into the groups occasionally for a random effect. When you have worked your way back to the original group of stalks, lift the nearest head and tuck the free ends of the last set of ropes underneath.

6 Make five more stalks with heads and arrange these so that their stalks lay over the first set, facing in the opposite direction. Trim some of these last stalks quite short so that one or two of the ears of wheat lay on top of the wreath. Use the plastic drinking straw to make two holes right through the dough on the opposite side of the wreath to the corn. Model a mouse and position it on one side of the wreath.

7 Roll out the rest of the dough to 3mm ($\frac{1}{8}$in) thick and use the wide strip cutter to cut out two 10cm (4in) long strips. Wrap these around the bunches of wheat at the bottom of the wreath so that they go between the two groups and tuck them under the edges of the wreath. Cut two more 10cm (4in) strips of dough and make a bow with long streamers, see page 13. Secure this on one of the binding strips and arrange the streamers so that they lay naturally on top of the ears of corn.

8 Finally, push a large hanging hook into the top of the wreath. Paint the whole wreath with the egg glaze and bake at 145°C (290°F/ Gas 1$\frac{1}{2}$) for about 3 hours. If you want a richer colour, continue to paint on egg glaze at regular intervals during the baking.

Painting and Finishing

Mix equal amounts of Cadmium Red and Yellow to make a bright orange and paint the binding ribbon and bow on the wreath.

Make some very watery Cadmium Red and wash a little of this onto the mouse's nose, tail and ear linings. Mark his eyes and paint his whiskers with Jet Black.

Varnish the wreath in the usual way and allow it to dry. Cut the ribbon in two and notch one end of each piece. Push the notched ends through the holes at the top of the wreath and tie a bow on the front. Take one of the ends hanging from the back of the wreath and wrap the ribbon around the wreath once or twice, making sure that you avoid any stray ears of wheat and the mouse. Fix the end of the ribbon onto the back of the wreath with a piece of Blu-Tack just above the bunches of wheat. Wind the other end of ribbon around the other side of the wreath in a similar manner.

To decorate the wreath with dried flowers, push a fairly large piece of Blu-Tack onto the painted bow and stick the stalks of the dried flowers into this. Cut the stalks fairly short so that the heads cover the Blu-Tack.

Thanksgiving Wreath

CHARACTERS

I have only included two people in this section, both children; however, the possibilities are, of course, limitless and the basic techniques remain the same regardless of the person you are making.

I have made Victorian bathing belles, a series of London street criers, fishermen, ballet dancers, grandmas and grandpas, and even a complete football team, and I am sure that you will feel equally inspired once you get going.

The animals are good fun, too, but I have not been commissioned to make quite such a broad variety of them. Come to think of it, though, I did make an elephant once and there was that penguin . . .

·VICTORIAN GIRL·

½ quantity Basic Dough, see page 10
7.5cm (3in) round fluted cutter
wooden skewer
cocktail sticks (toothpicks)
large and small rose cutters
garlic press or clay gun
fine sieve • hairpin

1   To make the legs, roll out two slim ropes of dough approximately 10cm (4in) long. Gently roll your finger 2cm ($\frac{3}{4}$ in) from the ends of each rope, making slight indentations. Dampen these, then push the ends of the dough up to form feet. Fix two very thin ropes around the legs, above the ankles, for boot tops. Trim the leg tops on the slant and place on a baking sheet.

2   Roll out three-quarters of the remaining dough, then cut out a fluted circle and make a frill, see page 14. Cut two short lengths of frill and fix them a little way up the legs to represent the lower edges of long bloomers.

3   To make the body, mould a small handful of dough into an oval shape approximately 5.5 × 3cm ($2\frac{1}{4}$ × $1\frac{1}{4}$ in). Place the body on the baking sheet and fix the tops of the legs to it.

4   Make another frill to represent a petticoat, then lay it across the legs, fixing it in place with a little water, and attach the ends to the sides of the legs. Do not attach the petticoat frill to the waist as this makes the model too bulky.

5   Measure your doll from the body top to just above the lower edge of the petticoat frill. Then roll out some dough and cut a piece almost as long as the measurement, by approximately 17.5cm (7in) wide. Taper one end of the dough so that it is slightly narrower at the top than the bottom. Make two small pleats at the top of the dough, facing each other in the middle. Fix these in place. Use a well-floured rolling pin to roll the top edge flat. This should give the effect of a slightly gathered bodice.

6   Dampen the body edges and the petticoat frill; lay the 'dress' on them, tucking it under the body and side of the frill. Hide the petticoat top but reveal its frill by fluting the dress.

7   Make two slim ropes, slightly thinner than the legs and about 7cm ($2\frac{3}{4}$ in) long for arms. Shape hands at one end of each, see page 13, and trim the other ends on the slant. Cut two short, narrow strips of rolled-out dough

Victorian Girl and George

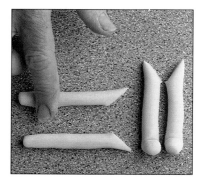

Victorian Girl

*Roll your finger just above the ends
of the legs to shape ankles, then
dampen them and push up the ends
of the dough to shape the feet.*

CRAFT TIP

You can always paint your
doll's clothes in colours you
have available. Try to keep to
my suggestion for the face,
though, and do not be
tempted to buy a tube of
paint labelled 'Flesh Colour'
. . . it won't be!

---

and fix them around the wrists to represent
cuffs. Attach the arms to the body.

8   Make a miniature doll in a similar way,
about 4cm (1½ in) high. Omit details, such as
fingers and petticoat, but mark the eyes and
mouth with a cocktail stick (toothpick) and
add a tiny ball of dough for the nose. Dampen
the back of the doll and lay it in position. Use
the end of a damp brush to lift the girl's hand
and gently bring the whole arm around to
cover the doll. Lift the other hand in the
same way and lay it against her dress, then
cover most of this hand with a small square of
dough to represent a pocket.

9   Fix another wide frill about 4cm (1½ in)
above the dress hem to represent a pinafore.
Use a cocktail stick (toothpick) to mark ribbon holes across the upper edge of the frill.
Arrange two thinner pieces of frill across the
shoulders and meeting at the front. Using the
smallest rose cutter, cut out a circle of dough
and cut it in half, then fix both halves to the top
of the dress to represent a collar.

10   Mould a ball of dough for the head and
mark the eyes and mouth with a cocktail stick
(toothpick). Add a small ball of dough for the
nose. Make the girl's hair by pressing dough
through a garlic press or clay gun. Push some
dough through a fine sieve for the doll's hair,
see page 13.

11   Using a large rose cutter, cut a circle and
attach it to the head for the brim of the hat. Use
a thicker piece of dough to cut a smaller circle
for the crown and attach it to the brim. Trim
the hat with ribbons made from two narrow
strips of dough and a tiny rosebud, see page 15.

12   Make another rosebud and two buttons
for the dress. Make bootlaces from very thin
ropes of dough. Finally push a whole hairpin
through the hat and into the head and body,
leaving just enough protruding to use as a
hanging hook. Bake at 145°C (290°F/Gas
1½) for about 2½ hours.

Painting and Finishing

●   Mix some white to a creamy consistency
and thoroughly mix in a very little touch of
Cadmium Yellow. Add a very small amount of
Cadmium Red to make a good flesh colour:
more a creamy beige than pink.

Paint the face and, while it is still wet, add a
little more red and white to some of the mix
and blend in to the cheeks. Paint the mouth
with a slightly darker version of this and the
eyes with a mixture of Ultramarine and white.
Use the rest of the flesh colour to paint the
hands and the arms, and face of the doll. Use
Spectrum Violet and white to mix the colour
for the dress, hat bands and ribbons.
Spectrum Violet is also used for the stockings
and buttons. Paint the pinafore a mixture of
Red Ochre and white. Decorate, when dry,
with a mix of Alizarin Crimson and white for
the flowers and Ultramarine, Cadmium
Yellow and white for the leaves.

Paint the frills and stripes white. A mixture
of Alizarin Crimson and white is used to tint
the roses, doll's cheeks and pinafore ribbons.
Paint the hat and boots with Raw Umber.

The doll's dress is Cadmium Yellow with
black spots. Add black shoes. Her hair is a
Cadmium Yellow and Cadmium Red mix;
eyes and stockings, Ultramarine and white.

·GEORGE·

½ quantity Basic Dough, see page 10
cocktail stick (toothpick)
old retractable ballpoint pen
medium rose cutter • garlic press

1   Make legs and feet as for Victorian Girl,
left, making socks instead of boots. Cut two
pieces of rolled-out dough, approximately 5

× 4cm (2 × 1in). Use a cocktail stick (tooth-pick) to carefully roll indentations across the wide side, then make these into creases by pressing them together a little. Use the back of a knife to mark the ribbing around the top edge of the socks. Dampen the legs just above the shoes and wrap the socks around them.

2   Cut out two more oblongs of dough 6.5 × 5cm (2½ × 2in) and fit these around the legs to represent trousers. Cut the tops of the legs, including trousers, on the slant and lay together on a baking sheet. Make the body and attach the legs as for Victorian Girl.

3   To make the sweater, cut a piece of rolled-out dough approximately 12.5 × 6.5cm (5 × ½ in). Taper the sides slightly so that the dough fits neatly on the shoulders. Use the back of a knife to mark the ribbing along the bottom edge. Fix the sweater so that it tucks under the body and covers the top of the trousers.

4   Make the arms as for the Victorian Girl and mark ribs on the cuffs. For the skate-board, cut out a long oval about 5 × 2cm (2 × ¾ in) and attach four flattened balls of dough for wheels. Indent the centre of each wheel with the old pen. Fix the skateboard against the body. Use a damp brush to pick up the boy's right hand and carefully arrange it over the skateboard. Lay the other hand against the trousers and cover most of it with a small square of dough to represent a pocket.

5   Make the head and hair as for the Victorian Girl. Arrange a narrow strip of dough around the neck to represent a collar.

6   Using the rose cutter, cut out a circle of dough and place it on the head. Press a small ball of dough down over half the circle so that the other half protrudes to represent the peak of the cap. Finish by arranging a fringed strip of dough around the shoulders and down the front to represent a scarf. Bake at 145°C (290°F/Gas 1½) for about 2½ hours.

Painting and Finishing

●   Paint the face, hands and legs as for the Victorian Girl, see page 46, adding a little mud and grime to his knees! Use a mix of Lamp Black and white to make a medium grey for the trousers and socks. Paint the sweater in a mixture of Ultramarine and white. Add the pattern using a fine brush and pure Cadmium Red, Cadmium Yellow and white. The green dots, stripes on socks and Tartan are a mixture of Ultramarine, Cadmium Yellow and white.

The base coat for the tartan is pure Red Ochre. When dry, use a fine brush to draw vertical lines in pure Cadmium Yellow, radiating from the centre of the cap; cross these with horizontal lines in the same colour and allow to dry before painting green lines between the vertical yellow ones. Repeat between the horizontal lines.

Paint the skateboard and the shoes Raw Umber and when dry, mark the lines on the board in red and white, and the laces of the shoes in black and white. Paint the wheels on the board in black with a white circle in the middle of each. Add a couple more red and blue stripes to the socks.

·CATHERINE SHEEP·

½ quantity Basic Dough, see page 10
modelling tool
Hanging Hook, see page 17
50cm (20in) pale pink ribbon

1   Roll a small piece of dough into four pencil-thin 7.5cm (3in) long ropes, see page 11.

2   Using a sharp knife, make a small cut at one end of each rope to represent hooves. Trim the other ends on the slant and fix

George
Using tweezers to tranfer George's hair from the garlic press to his head.

CRAFT TIP

Painting tartan looks and sounds difficult but it is, in fact, really easy, so have a go.

Catherine Sheep
You need between 60 and 70 coils of dough to build up Catherine's wool.

them together, in pairs, with a little water. Lay the pairs of legs close together on a baking sheet.

3 Knead and mould another piece of dough into an oval shape measuring approximately 8 × 5.5cm ($3\frac{3}{4}$ × $2\frac{1}{4}$in). Fix this over the tops of the legs, leaving the hooves and legs extending by 4cm ($1\frac{1}{2}$in).

4 Take a walnut-sized piece of dough and pinch it into a face shape. Mark the eyes and nostrils with the sharp end of the modelling tool, then fix it to one end of the body. Using the rounded end of the modelling tool, form two very small balls of dough into cup shapes to represent ears and attach them to the head.

5 Roll out several very thin ropes of dough and cut them into 5cm (2in) lengths. Roll each length into a coil: you will need between 60 and 70 coils to make the sheep's wool.

6 Dampen the sheep, then attach the coils in a higgledy-piggledy fashion all over the head and body. Stick a few coils on top of each other to build up the tail.

7 Attach a hanging hook and use the modelling tool to make a hole just behind the head. The hole is to thread a ribbon through when the sheep is finished. Bake at 145°C (290°F/Gas $1\frac{1}{2}$) for approximately 2 hours.

Painting and Finishing

● Use a medium brush to paint the legs and face Lamp Black. Carefully drag some watery white paint over the sheep's coat, so that some of the natural dough colour shows through and gives it some depth.

Add a little speck of Alizarin Crimson to the watery white to paint the ear linings and nostrils. Use a mixture of Ultramarine and white for the eyes. Allow to dry, then varnish. When the varnish is dry, thread the ribbon through the neck hole and tie in a bow.

·HEATHCLIFF PIG·

The quantity of dough below is sufficient to make two pigs.
$\frac{1}{2}$ quantity Basic Dough, see page 10
modelling tool
large briar rose cutter
Hanging Hook, see page 17

1 Make four legs following steps 1 and 2 as for the Sheep, left. The legs should be slightly thinner than those for the sheep and they should be 5cm (2in) long.

2 Knead a small handful of dough and mould it into a flattened circle of 7.5cm (3in) in diameter. Fix this over the top of the legs leaving 3cm ($1\frac{3}{4}$in) uncovered.

3 For the head, flatten a piece of dough into a 5cm (2in) circle. Fix it in place on the body. Flatten a small ball of dough to approximately 2cm ($\frac{3}{4}$in) across for the snout. Fix it in position, then use the modelling tool to mark the nostrils and eyes.

4 Roll out a small quantity of dough thinly and use the large briar rose cutter to cut out two ears. Attach these in place on the head.

5 Make a thin rope, approximately 7.5cm (3in) long, and attach one end to the pig's rear end. Give the rope a twist, then fix the other end against the body. Fix a hanging hook in the pig's back and bake at 145°C (290°F/Gas $1\frac{1}{2}$) for about 1 hour.

Painting and Finishing

● If you have not already baked the pink colour into the pig, wash some very watery Alizarin Crimson over the tummy, cheeks and feet. Use a medium brush and Lamp Black to paint uneven patches on the pig's sides and ears. Paint the eyes with the same colour. Allow to dry, then varnish.

Heathcliff Pig, see page 50, and Catherine Sheep

Finley Fish

·FINLEY FISH·

$\frac{1}{4}$ quantity Paste Dough, see page 10
Fish Template, see page 139
thin card • rose cutters
old retractable ballpoint pen
Hanging Hook, see page 17

1 Roll out half the dough to 6mm ($\frac{1}{2}$ in) thick. Flour the template, place on the dough and cut around it with a sharp knife. Lay the fish carefully on a baking tray and smooth any rough edges.

2 Roll out the remaining dough thinly. Then, using the small, medium and large rose cutters, cut out an assortment of circles. You need approximately 23 very small; 23 medium; and 17 large circles. Dampen the fish and, starting at the base of the tail, begin arranging circles in overlapping rows. Begin with two rows of small circles, followed by two rows of medium, three rows of large, a further two rows of medium and finally two rows of small circles. This arrangement should take you up to the head of the fish which is left plain.

3 Place a tiny ball of dough in position for an eye and mark the centre with the old ballpoint pen. Join a small, thin rope of dough into a tiny circle for the mouth.

CRAFT TIP

Add two or three coats of varnish to enhance this model and make it glitter and shine

52

Claude and Cat Napping, see page 74

53

4 Use the back of a knife and the retracted pen to decorate the tail fin and head. Fix a hanging hook in position and bake at 145°C (290°F/Gas 1½) for about 1½ hours.

Painting and Finishing

● Make up very thin washes of Magenta, Ultramarine, and Viridian. Mix Magenta and white to make a pale pink, also make a wash of this.

Brush the fish with water. Using a large soft brush, run the pink along the stomach. Do the same with the Magenta wash working a little higher up the body, then use the Ultramarine wash above the Magenta. Finally, wash on the Viridian at the very top and allow the colours to mingle. You can encourage the mingling a little with a clean brush but do not mix the colours too much or they will become muddy.

When the paint is almost dry take some silver paint on a dry brush and drag it across the top scales of the fish so that it lands in uneven patches and catches the light, like real scales. Allow to dry and varnish.

·CLAUDE·

The quantity of dough makes two cats.
½ quantity Basic Dough, see page 10
modelling tool • small rose cutter
Hanging Hook, see page 17

1 Take a small piece of well-kneaded dough and mould it into four 6.5cm (2½ in) pencil-thin ropes, see page 11.

2 Flatten one end of each rope slightly, then make four small cuts along the flat edge to represent toes. Round-off each toe with a damp brush. Follow the instructions for Heathcliff Pig, see page 50, to the end of step 3.

3 Flatten two small balls of dough and fix

them to the face to make whisker pads. The pads should be touching and they look more realistic if you use a damp brush and a modelling tool to smooth their upper edges into the face. Form a tiny piece of dough into a triangular-shaped nose and fix it in place between the tops of the pads.

4 Roll out a small amount of dough thinly and use the rose cutter to cut out a small circle. Cut this into quarters so that you have four wedges. Use only two wedges: press them out slightly with your fingers and fix them in position for the ears.

5 Cut a thin strip of dough, long enough to fit around the cat's neck. Attach this with a little water before adding a bow, see page 13.

6 Make a 7.5cm (3in) rope for the tail and fix it in place. Attach a hanging hook and bake at 145°C (290°F/Gas 1½) for about 1 hour.

Painting and Finishing

● Mix a little Raw Umber and white together, and paint everything except the bow and the parts that are going to be white. Using Raw Umber, white and Lamp Black, mix a lighter brown, a darker brown and black. Using these three colours alternately, paint tabby markings all over the face and the body, with a striped effect on the legs and tail. Paint the tip of the tail, face, bib and paws white, and, while this is still damp, mix a little Alizarin Crimson and white together, then blend the pink on his whisker pads and toes. The ear linings may also be tinted pink.

Paint the eye shapes Sap Green, then add the pupil and outline in black. The bow is a mixture of Ultramarine and white, spotted with white. I have added a few black dots to the whisker pads but be very delicate with these or they can look a bit grotesque.

CRAFT TIP

If your passion is for ginger cats, mix Golden Yellow and Rose Malmaison for a wonderful colour.

·BEAR PORTRAITS·

½ quantity Paste Dough, see page 10
medium and small rose cutters
modelling tool
old retractable ballpoint pen

1 Roll out a quarter of the dough medium thick, cut out a rectangle measuring 7.5 × 6.5cm (3 × 2½ in) and lay it on a baking sheet. Take a smooth walnut-sized ball of dough and mould one side into an oval for the bear's nose. Dampen the other side of the dough and fix it in the middle of the rectangle. Flatten two small balls of dough and place them side by side on the extreme point of the oval to make whisker pads. Fix a very small triangle of dough, point downwards, at the top of the pads for a nose.

2 Mould a small piece of dough into a rough semi-circle about 6.5cm (2½ in) wide by about 4cm (1½ in) deep. Arrange this on the rectangle, under the head so that the curved side forms shoulders. Trim off any excess.

MR BEAR

3 Cut two oblongs of rolled-out dough 2.5 × 12mm (1 × ½ in). Fix them on either side of the bear's neck, turning the front upper corners back to form a winged collar. Drape a very small, thin square of dough in the opening of his collar and down his chest to represent a cravat. Place a very small ball of dough on this for a tie-pin.

4 For jacket lapels, cut two oblongs of rolled-out dough measuring 4cm × 12mm (1½ × ½ in). Notch these, halfway along the long side and fix them in position.

5 Use the medium rose cutter to cut out a circle for the hat brim. Add a small ball of dough for the crown and place the hat on top

Bear Portraits

Bear Portraits
Adding the whisker pads.

of the bear's head. Mould two small balls of dough and, using the rounded end of the modelling tool, flatten them into saucer-shaped ears. Arrange these on either side of the hat so that they curl the rim up slightly. Follow steps 9–12 to finish and bake.

MRS BEAR

6   Follow steps 1 and 2. Make a 5cm (2in) frill, see page 14, and arrange it around the neck. Make two more frills, 4cm (1½in) long and arrange them over the shoulders, almost meeting in the middle.

7   Make two ears, following step 5, and fix these to the head. Cut a small circle for the hat brim and arrange this at a slight angle over one ear. Use a small rose cutter and a slightly thicker piece of dough to make the crown and fix it on the brim with a little water. Cut two small strips for ribbons and arrange them at the back of the hat.

8   Make two small rosebuds, see page 15, then fix one in the hat and one at Mrs Bear's throat.

9   Make two pencil-thin ropes of dough, see page 11, each about 30cm (12in) long. Dampen the edges of the rectangle and encircle it with one rope, joining the ends on a corner and smoothing the join with the modelling tool.

10   Coil the second rope from both ends so that both coils meet in the middle. Fix the coils in this position with a little water, then attach the double coil to the bottom of the frame, with the coils downwards. Mould a 7.5cm (3in) length of rope into a circle and fix this in the middle of the top of the frame.

11   Mould two 7.5cm (3in) ropes and make a single coil at both ends of each rope. Arrange these around the circle so that two coils meet back to back at the top of the circle and the remaining coils are attached to the frame.

12   Mark a pattern in all the ropes using the old pen. Bake at 145°C (290°F/Gas 1½) for 2 hours.

Painting and Finishing

Mr Bear Carefully wash some very watery Red Ochre over the background. When dry, add thin white stripes – or even floral wallpaper – keeping the colours very transparent or they will detract from the portrait.

Paint the face with thin Yellow Ochre, adding just a blush of Red Ochre to the cheeks. Paint the shirt and collar white and make two white almond shapes for eyes. Paint the left eye first if you are right handed so that your hand does not get in the way when you are trying to match the eyes. Reverse the process, of course, if you are left handed.

Use some pure Raw Umber to paint the hat and the base coat for the jacket. When dry, add a little white to the umber and use a very fine brush to paint the herring bone design. The cravat is painted with Permanent Green Middle and spotted with white.

Take a very fine brush and paint the inverted 'V' between the whisker pads with Raw Umber. Use the same colour to paint the irises in the eyes. Outline the eyes and paint his nose and whisker dots in Lamp Black. Black may be used for the shirt stripes but blue looks better.

Paint the frame first with a good creamy mixture of Red Ochre, then, when dry, take some Gold on a dry brush and drag it over the red. Leave as much of the red showing through as you like to make the frame look more distressed, like an old gilded frame.

Mrs Bear Paint the background and the face as for Mr Bear, except, perhaps, adding a slightly more feminine blush around her nose and in her ears. Paint the roses and frills with Permanent White and tint the edges of the roses slightly with thin Alizarin Crimson.

The dress is a mixture of Spectrum Violet and white, decorated with pure Spectrum Violet flowers. I have used the fatal-sounding Permanent Green Middle to paint the ribbons on the hat and the centres of the flowers. The rest of the hat and the frame are painted with Red Ochre, and the frame is finished with Gold.

· HALLOWEEN WITCH ·

If your family is like mine and never actually manages to achieve any of the idyllic stuff connected with seasonal festivities, but tends to go straight for the foul fiends, you might like to spend halloween making this wicked little witch and her jet-lagged cat.

¾ quantity Basic Dough, see page 10
garlic press or clay gun, or both if possible
plastic ruler
cocktail stick (toothpick)
modelling tool
5cm (2in) and 12mm (½in) round cutters
2 Hanging Hooks, see page 17

1 Roll out a finger-thick rope of dough 22.5cm (9in) long. Place this on a baking tray at a slight angle and score it lightly with a knife to represent bark.

2 If you have a clay gun it is better to use this instead of a garlic press for the twigs of the broom. It is easier to extrude long strands and it gives the dough a better texture. I have used the gun for the twigs and the garlic press for the hair to accentuate the difference. Build up 10cm (4in) lengths of dough from the clay gun over the right-hand end of the broom handle to make a thick bunch of twigs. Dent the twigs slightly about 6mm (¼in) from the end of the broom handle and lay several very thin ropes of dough over the dent to represent binding.

3 Make two 12.5cm (5in) pencil-thin ropes of dough for legs, tapering one end of each to a point. Flatten 2.5cm (1in) of the pointed ends with your finger to make feet. Roll two very thin 2.5cm (1in) ropes of dough and wrap them around the legs just above the feet to look like boot tops. Arrange the legs, one under, and the other over, the broomstick, then fix them with a little water.

4 Model an oval of dough for the body and attach it to the broomstick so that it appears to be leaning forward slightly. Then take half the remaining dough and roll it out to about 3mm (⅛in) thick. Using a well-floured ruler and a sharp knife, cut out a triangle measuring 17.5cm (7in) across the base and 10cm (4in) high. Trim 12mm (½in) from the apex of the triangle, then drape it around the witch's body like a dress, fitting the blunted apex around the neck and tucking the sides under.

5 Roll out two thin ropes for arms making hands at one end of them and trimming the other ends at a slant, see page 13. Fit the slanting ends to the body and rest the hands on the broomstick.

6 Cut a triangle for the cloak, making it 15cm (6in) across the base and 10cm (4in) high. Trim 12mm (½in) from the apex of the triangle as before, then drape it over the back of the witch so that it covers the join where the front arm meets the body. The cloak should appear to billow out behind the witch. Fold back the nearest edge of the cloak and cut two thin strips of dough to use as ties at the front. Arrange these to look knotted.

7 Fit a ball of dough on the shoulders to represent the head and model a grinning mouth with a modelling tool. Fit a tiny ball of dough into the mouth for the one, and only, tooth and make a wedge-shaped piece of dough into a nose. Use a cocktail stick (tooth-pick) to make two small, close-set eyes. Press dough through a garlic press to make hair, see page 12, and arrange it flying back.

8 Cut out a 5cm (2in) circle of dough and place it on the witch's head for the brim of her hat. To make the top of the hat, cut a triangle of rolled-out dough measuring 7.5cm (3in) across the base and 5cm (2in) high. Bend this into a conical shape, joining the edges with a little water. Fit the cone of dough on top of the brim with the join at the back and add a narrow strip of dough for a hat band.

9 Model a small oval of dough for the cat's body and sit this up behind the witch. Roll two short thin ropes of dough for the cat's legs, making the back one slightly thicker at one end to represent his haunch. Cut three little toes at the paw ends and fix the legs in place on the body. Make a short, slightly pointed, rope for the cat's tail and a small ball for his head.

10 Cut a 12mm ($\frac{1}{2}$in) circle of rolled-out dough and cut it into quarters. Use two of these quarters for ears and a very small ball of dough for a nose. Place two very small flattened balls of dough side by side under the cat's nose for whisker pads and add a strip of dough for a collar and a bow, see page 14.

11 Fix a hanging hook in the twiggy end of the broom and another in the hat. Bake at 145°C (290°F/Gas 1$\frac{1}{2}$) for about 2$\frac{1}{2}$ hours.

Painting and Finishing

● Mix up flesh colour and paint the witch's face and hands, see page 42. As she is obviously quite a fashion-conscious witch, I have added a little more Cadmium Red to her 'blusher' and also painted some lipstick and a beauty spot. Remember to paint her tooth!

Paint the dress, boots, hat band and the cat's bow in Viridian and allow to dry. Add golden stars, moons and planets to the dress, and spots to the hat band and the cat's bow.

Paint the cloak a rich Magenta. Paint the cat, the witch's stockings and her hat Jet Black. Finish the cat by adding a little watery Magenta to the whisker pads, inside the ears and the paws.

Mix Cadmium Red and Cadmium Yellow together, adding slightly more yellow. Paint the witch's mane of red hair. Paint a wash of Raw Umber on the broom handle and on the binding.

Halloween Witch

1 quantity Basic Dough, see page 10
7.5cm (3in) round fluted cutter
cocktail stick (toothpick)
5cm (2in) and 2.5cm (1in) round cutters
fine floristry wire
smallest round cutter from carnation set

1 Take a small handful of dough and make two 10cm (4in) long, pencil-thin ropes. Trim one end of each diagonally and make two small cuts in the opposite ends to represent toes.

2 Model a second handful of dough into an oval shape measuring about 5.5×3cm ($2\frac{1}{4} \times 1\frac{1}{4}$in). Lay the oval vertically on a baking tray and secure the mitred ends of the legs to either side at the bottom of it.

3 Roll out half the remaining dough to 3mm ($\frac{1}{8}$in) thick and cut a 20×7.5cm (8×3in) strip. Lay this horizontally on the work surface and trim the bottom edge so that it is very slightly curved. Wet a spot in the middle of the top edge and, lifting the right-hand side of the dough, fold about 5cm (2in) of it onto the damp spot to make a pleat. Do the same with the left-hand side so that you have two pleats facing each other. Dust a little flour along the top edge of the strip to soak up any dampness, then roll the top 2.5cm (1in) of the dough so that the top of the pleats are flattened. Trim off any uneven dough.

4 Drape the strip across the lower half of the rabbit, so that the pleated edge is on her waist. Tuck the sides under and arrange the dough so that the skirt flares at the bottom and fits into her waist at the top.

5 Make two 7.5cm (3in) long ropes for the arms. Cut both ends diagonally as for legs. Fit the diagonal ends to the body and leave the arms out to the side for the time being.

6 To make the bottom of the apron, cut a 5cm (2in) square from the rolled-out dough. Trim two of the corners to make a curved shape at the bottom, then fit the straight edge around her waist. Cut out a circle with the fluted cutter and frill the edges with the cocktail stick (toothpick), see page 14. Use the 5cm (2in) round cutter to cut out the centre of the fluted circle, then use the remaining frill to trim the edges of the apron. Make a few holes around the inner edge of the frill so that you can paint on ribbon later. Finish the apron with a little pocket.

7 Cut a 3cm ($1\frac{1}{4}$in) square of rolled-out dough and attach it to the rabbit's chest to represent the bib of an apron. Make some more frilling and fit a strip along the right-hand side of the bib and over the shoulder. Arrange the left-hand side to match.

8 Cut out a 2.5cm (1in) circle of rolled-out dough and cut it in half. Use these two semi-circles to make a collar for the top of the dress. Model a small piece of dough into an oval shape for the head and place it on top of the collar with the pointed end foremost. Use the cocktail stick (toothpick) to make nostrils.

9 Cut two long leaf shapes of a similar size and model these into ears by curling in the edges a little. Fit the ears on the head. Cut out the lace cap with the small carnation cutter and make several ribbon holes around the edge before securing it on the head between the ears. Cut two long strips with notched ends and fix these under the cap, then between the ears and out to one side of the head.

10 Cut six short lengths of floristry wire and stick three of these into the dough on either side of her nose to represent whiskers. Fix a thin strip of dough around either wrist to represent cuffs. Finish these off by adding a button made from a little ball of dough.

11 Make a little head for the baby, without whiskers and nostrils, with a little nose instead. Fit the head on a small oval of dough. Cut out a circle of dough with the fluted cutter and wrap it around the baby rabbit to make a shawl. Lay the baby on the rabbit's chest and put her arms around it, securing the paws with a little water.

12 Make ribbon holes around the shawl edge and prick it all over with a cocktail stick. Flatten a little oval ball of dough for the nanny's brooch.

Painting and Finishing

● Mix up quite a strong blue by adding a little white to some Ultramarine. Paint the nanny's dress with this and dry for a few minutes before painting the stripes in a watery white. Keeping the white fairly thin, but opaque, paint the shawl, apron, cuffs, collar and cap. Allow to dry.

Paint the ribbons on the apron and cap, and the buttons on the cuffs in pure Alizarin. Add a little white to the dress colour and then paint the ribbon on the shawl. Mix a little Raw Umber and white together, and use this to paint the nanny's face and paws. Blend a little watery Alizarin into the tips of her paws, nose, nostrils and ears before the brown is thoroughly dry. Paint her eyes.

Add a little more white to the brown. Starting close to her nose, paint a wedge shape skirting the upper edges of her eyes and ending at the outer corners of her ears. Use the same brown to paint the baby rabbit, blending a little watery Alizarin inside his ears and on his nose.

Take a very fine brush and black to paint closed eyes on the baby and a heart-shaped nose on the nanny. Paint the nanny's brooch black and her whiskers white.

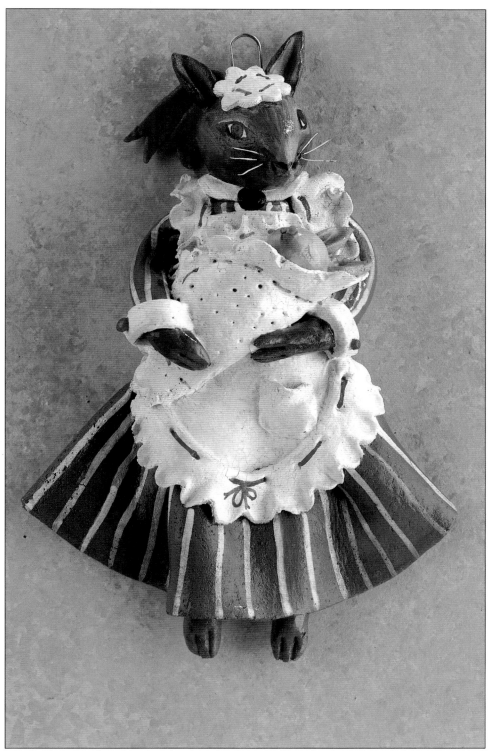

Nanny Rabbit and Baby Rabbit

61

· *BRIDAL COUPLE* ·

This is another model where it is tempting to make the characters look like the real couple. This need not be too difficult if, for example, the bridegroom is undeniably short and fat or unbelievably tall and thin, or if the bride has masses of curly, red hair and is known to be lavish with the eye shadow. However, whatever they look like, you can still have fun by giving your bridal pair imaginative expressions.

1¼ quantities Basic Dough, see page 10
cocktail stick (toothpick)
2.5cm (1in) and 12mm (½in) round cutters
blossom plunger cutter
garlic press
15cm (6in) saucer
retracted ballpoint pen

1 Take a handful of well-kneaded dough and make two 11.5cm (4½in) long, finger-thick ropes for the groom's legs. If you have to trim the ropes to size, leave one end of each rounded to form the feet. Set the legs aside. Roll out half the remaining dough to 3mm (⅛in) thick. Cut out two 9 × 7.5cm (3½ × 3in) rectangles and wrap them around the legs with the joins at the back and 12mm (½in) of the rounded end of the leg protruding. Secure the rectangles to the back of the legs with a little water before laying them side by side on a baking tray.

2 Model a suitably sized piece of dough into a ball for the groom's body and attach it to the top of the legs. Cut two triangles with 5cm (2in) sides from the rolled-out dough and slightly round each of the corners with a knife. Arrange these on either side of the

groom's body so that they meet in the middle to resemble a V-necked waistcoat and tuck any spare dough around the back of the body. The waistcoat should cover the join between the body and the top of the legs. Place three very small balls of dough along the seam where the triangles meet, to represent buttons.

3 Make a ball for the head and place it on the body, marking the eyes and mouth with a cocktail stick (toothpick). Attach a tiny ball of dough for a nose. Secure two small strips of dough around his neck so that they stand up like a wing collar.

4 Cut a triangle with a 4cm (1½in) base and 6.5cm (2½in) sides. Round off the left-hand side of the base before turning the triangle upside down and fitting it over the right-hand shoulder of the model (*his* right-hand shoulder). This piece represents one side of the coat, so pull it back slightly to reveal the waistcoat and tuck any spare dough away behind the body again. Cut a small tapered strip for the lapel and cut a notch in it, then secure it on the front of the coat with a little water. Make the other side of the coat in a similar way, taking care to show sufficient of the waistcoat as this is going to be his *pièce de résistance* when painted.

5 Make an arm about 9cm (3½in) long with a left hand, see page 13. Wrap a 6.5 × 2.5cm (2½ × 1in) strip around the bottom of the arm for a shirt cuff. Cut a 6cm (2½in) square for the coat sleeve and fit it around the arm in a similar way to the trouser legs, leaving some of the shirt cuff showing. Trim the top of the arm diagonally and fit it on the left side of the body with a little water.

6 Cut out a 2.5cm (1in) circle for the hat brim. Then model the crown by making a ball and shaping it slightly. Fix the crown onto the brim with a little water, then tuck the hat under his arm so that his hand curves under-

---

CRAFT TIP

Even though dough dolls have extremely simple features, it is amazing how much expression you can show by altering their size and position. A baby-faced person, for example, usually has large eyes set far apart with a small nose and mouth quite close to each other. For a more lugubrious expression, you could try making the head more oval, then put the eyes closer together and leave a greater space between the nose and the mouth. Alternatively, you could just model suitable noses when you are making the dolls and paint the rest of the features when they are cooked, see page 17.

neath to support it. Make a generous bow tie for the groom, see page 13, and cut out a blossom for his button hole. Finally, give him some garlic-press hair, see page 12, and add a few dough buttons to his coat and sleeve.

7 Knead all the scraps of dough left from the groom into the remains of the original ball. You may have to add a little water, but knead the dough for 2 to 3 minutes until it is pliable and smooth again. Make a pair of far slimmer, 10cm (4in) long legs for the bride. Keep one end of each rounded and trim the other ends diagonally. Place these on a baking tray beside the groom.

8 Make a small oval body about 4.5cm ($1\frac{3}{4}$in) tall for the bride and attach it to the legs so that the diagonals fit around either side at one end. Then give her a little bust by attaching two small balls of dough close together on her chest.

9 Roll out half the remaining dough to 3mm ($\frac{1}{8}$in) thick. Cut out a triangle with a 20cm (8in) base and 15cm (6in) high sides. Carefully cut scallops along the base of the triangle before indenting a pattern around them with the retracted ballpoint pen. Use the blossom plunger cutter to indent a little flower on every scallop. Cut 2.5cm (1in) from the apex of the triangle, then place it just under the bustline. Drape the rest of the dress around the bride, turning the two straight edges under by about 2.5cm (1in) and allowing one side to flow across the groom's trousers.

10 Make two 6.5cm ($2\frac{1}{2}$in) long arms with hands, see page 13, and make two cuffs by attaching tiny ropes of dough around each wrist. Attach the arms to the body as for the groom. Take a strip of dough measuring about 7.5 × 4.5cm (3 × $1\frac{3}{4}$in). Scallop and decorate this strip in the same way as the dress hem, then drape it across the bust and shoulders to form the top of the dress.

Bridal Couple

11 Make the bride's head as for the groom but do not give her any hair until you have completed the veil. To do this, cut out a circle of dough using the saucer as a template. Cut it in half and decorate the curved edge of one half using the retracted ballpoint pen and the cocktail stick (toothpick). Arrange the decorated half so that one end of the curved side is laying on the bride's head. Drape the rest of the veil so that it flies out behind the bride. Before permanently securing the veil, make some very long hair by pressing dough through the garlic press, see page 12, and tuck the ends of this up under the veil on top of the head. Trail the rest of the hair out across the veil, then secure the head-piece for the veil with a little water. Cut out some small flowers with the blossom plunger cutter and arrange them as a garland around the head-piece of the veil.

12 Use the small round cutter to make about eighteen small rosebuds, see page 15, and arrange them in the form of a bouquet on the front of the dress, placing the bride's hands around them. Add a few tapered strips of dough for leaves and several little balls of dough, pricked in the middle to represent some more tiny flowers. Finally, add two notched streamers of ribbon to the flower bouquet . . . and the couple are ready to be married.

13 Bake at 145°C (290°F/Gas 1½) for about 3 hours.

Painting and Finishing

● Mix up flesh colour and paint the faces and hands, see page 42. Then take some pure Jet Black and paint the groom's coat. Add a little white to make a dark grey for his trousers. Leave to dry before adding black stripes. You will find that the rigger brush will make this job far easier. Add white to the dark grey to make the pale colour for the groom's waistcoat and hat. Leave to dry for 1 to 2 minutes before painting the hat band in a slightly darker grey.

Make a large pool of diluted white, and paint the groom's shirt and the bride's veil, legs and dress. Paint the dress last so that it is still damp enough to blend a little pale pink into the scalloped edges. Make pink by adding the merest hint of Alizarin Crimson to the white. Add a tiny bit more Alizarin and paint some of the paler flowers on the groom's waistcoat and his button hole. You could also paint one or two

of the roses in the bride's bouquet and some of the flowers in her head-dress.

Take pure Alizarin and paint the groom's socks, bow tie and the remainder of the flowers on his waistcoat. Let the tie dry for 1 to 2 minutes then add some white dots.

When his socks are dry, paint on black shoes with pale grey laces. Then, while you have the grey on the brush, paint the buttons on his shirt front.

Mix a little Lemon Yellow and white to make a very pale yellow for some of the bride's roses and the centre of the groom's button hole. Add small amounts of Cadmium Red to this mixture to make a variety of pinks and oranges for the bride's roses and the flowers in her head-dress.

Take some pure Olive Green and paint the leaves in the bouquet, the buttons on the groom's waistcoat and some little dots in the middles of, and among, the flowers on his waistcoat.

Complete the bride's bouquet by painting the little balls of dough with a very pale green made from Lemon Yellow, white and a touch of Olive Green. Add a little Ultramarine to white to make the pale blue for the ribbons. Then trim her veil and paint her shoes in Gold.

MOTHER AND BABY
· WITH PRAM ·

$\frac{3}{4}$ quantity Basic Dough, see page 10
7.5cm (3in), 4cm (1½in) and 12mm (½in) round
cutters
large plastic drinking straw
small piece of kitchen foil
5cm (2in) round fluted cutter
cocktail stick (toothpick)
15cm (6in) saucer
garlic press
small blossom plunger cutter
3 Hanging Hooks, see page 17

1   Take a handful of dough and make a
22.5cm (9in) long, fairly thick rope. Flatten
this slightly with your fingers and lay it on a
baking tray.

2   Roll out half the remaining dough to 3mm
(⅛in) thick and cut out a 7.5cm (3in) circle.
Cut this in two so that one portion is a little
larger than the other. Put the larger half to one
side, with its curved side towards the bottom.
Cut the other piece in half. Secure one half on
the cut edge of the first piece to look like a
pram with a hood.

3   To make the wheel cut out a 4cm (1½in)
circle. Then, using the large plastic drinking
straw as a cutter, decorate this with eight holes
around the edge. Make a small round centrepiece for the wheel with the 12mm (½in)
cutter and secure it in place with a little
water. Indent the centre slightly with the
drinking straw.

4   Secure the wheel to the curved side of the
pram, so that half of it overlaps the body of the
pram. Then attach the whole pram at one end
of the flattened rope. Tuck a small roll of
kitchen foil under the unsupported half of
the wheel to prevent it sagging. Make a thin

Mother and Baby with Pram

5cm (2in) rope for the pram handle and,
curving the top end over slightly, secure this
in place at one end of the pram.

5   Using the 5cm (2in) fluted cutter, cut out
a circle and frill the edges, see page 14. Use
the cocktail stick (toothpick) to prick holes
around the edge inside the frill – these will be
used as eyelet holes for painted 'ribbon' at a
later stage. Carefully fold the frilled circle in
half and arrange it on top of the pram as a
coverlet.

6   Make a small ball of dough for the baby's
head and mark the eyes and mouth with a
cocktail stick (toothpick). Make a tiny ball

see page 13,

of dough for the nose and arrange a strip of dough and a bow, see page 13, around the head. Secure the head on top of the coverlet and against the hood of the pram.

7   Prepare two 10cm (4in) long pencil-slim legs for the mother and attach a thin rope around each of the ankles to represent the top of her boots. Secure one of her feet to the flattened rope and arrange the other leg so that it looks as though she is walking. Join her legs at the top with a little water. Model an oval body about 4cm (1½in) high and secure it to the top of her legs.

8   Roll out some more dough, if necessary, and cut out a large circle using the saucer as a template. Cut the top 2.5cm (1in) from the circle, then make a mark in the middle of the straight edge. Make two more marks about one third of the way down from the top around either side of the curve. Hold a ruler between the top mark and one mark on the curve and use it as a guide to cut off a section of dough. Do the same between the top mark and the second mark on the curve. Drape this round-bottomed wedge of dough over the body and legs of the mother so that the curved edge is at the bottom. Tuck the dough under on either side and arrange it so that it is slightly pleated and floating out behind her.

9   Make a 6.5cm (2½in) arm and left hand, see page 13. Wrap a 5cm (2in) square of dough around the arm to form a sleeve. Cut off the top of the arm diagonally and secure it to the body so that the hand reaches the handle of the pram.

10   Cut a little curved strip about 4cm (1½in) long to form the collar and place it around the top of the coat. Make a pocket from a 4cm (1½in) square of dough, with one side slightly curved. Dampen this around the edges and position it on the coat so that it bulges slightly.

Then prick around the edges with a cocktail stick (toothpick) to represent stitching.

11   Cut a thin 5cm (2in) long strip of dough for the belt and attach it on the back of the coat so that it folds under the outside edge a little. Make four tiny balls of dough for the buttons and flatten them slightly. Position three of them down the front of the coat and the fourth at one end of the belt. Make two holes in each button with the cocktail stick (toothpick).

12   Roll a ball of dough for the head and mark the eyes and mouth with a cocktail stick (toothpick). Attach a tiny ball of dough for the nose, then secure the head to the body so that it is slightly turned. Make some long hair with the garlic press and arrange this on the head so that, like the coat, it appears to be blowing backwards.

13   Model a small cylinder of dough for the crown of the hat and fix it on top of the mother's head. Cut out a 4cm (1½in) circle of dough and press it out slightly between your fingers and thumbs. Then fold it in half and fit it across the top of the front of the head, against the crown of the hat. Prick around the curved edge with the cocktail stick (toothpick) and decorate the hat with a few flowers made with the blossom cutter.

14   Finally, cover the flattened base rope with grass, made by pressing dough through the garlic press and picking out short lengths of dough. Dot several little flowers made with the blossom cutter among the grass. Put one hook in the mother's hat and one at either end of the base. Bake at 145°C (290°F/Gas 1½) for about 2 hours.

Painting and Finishing

●   Mix up some flesh colour and paint both the faces, see page 42. Add Red Ochre to some diluted white to make enough dusky pink to

see page 42.

CRAFT TIP

This model cannot be hung from the highest point, the mother's hat, because that is not in the centre and the model would hang at an angle. Sometimes you can put a second hook in the next highest point and solve the problem by threading hanging ribbon through the two hooks. That would look clumsy here because there is such a large gap between the hat and the hood on the pram. I put one hook in the hat, and a second and third at either end of the grass; so, two extra pins can be used to hold the model straight when hung.

paint the mother's coat. Allow this to dry. Then make up a mixture of Ultramarine and white for the horizontal and vertical, pale blue stripes. If possible, use a rigger brush to do this, see page 112. Allow the blue to dry.

Use a mixture of Lemon Yellow and white to put in the pale yellow checks, painting horizontal and vertical lines in between the blue ones.

Take some slightly diluted Red Ochre to paint the pram and the mother's hat, gloves and boots. Allow these to dry before using some of the pale yellow mixture and a fine brush or rigger to paint the design on the pram and one of the flowers in the mother's hat. Paint the other two flowers with some of the pale blue and pink left over from the coat.

Use pure Jet Black to paint the spokes and hub of the pram wheel, and the mother's legs. Allow the black to dry. Then trim the wheel with silver, using the same colour for the pram handle and the mother's coat buttons. Paint the centre of the wheel hub with a touch of Red Ochre.

Mix up quite a pool of Lemon Yellow, Olive Green and white to make the colour for the grass and apply it carefully, making sure that you get in all the nooks and crannies. When the grass is completely dry take some diluted white and paint some of the flowers and the coverlet on the pram.

When the coverlet is dry, add a little Cadmium Red to the white and paint the ribbon on the coverlet, the rest of the flowers and the baby's bow. Finish off by putting a little dot of yellow into the centre of each of the flowers.

· CAROL SINGERS ·

This Dickensian-looking group is a good example of the important role painting takes when trying to produce attractive dough models. The project takes some time to model and it would be truly awful to ruin it with a quick coat of the garish colours that are so often associated with dough modelling.

$1\frac{1}{4}$ quantities Basic Dough, see page 10
fine sieve · cocktail stick (toothpick)
5cm (2in) and 2.5cm (1in) round cutter
fine strip cutter
5cm (2in) fluted round cutter
small blossom plunger cutter
garlic press or clay gun
retracted ballpoint pen
3 Hanging Hooks, see page 17

1 Take a handful of dough and roll it into a fat rope, about 17.5cm (7in) long. Lay this on a baking tray. Make two 6.5cm (2½in) long ropes for legs and shape quite large shoes at their ends, see page 13; put these to one side.
2 Roll out half of the remaining dough to 3mm ($\frac{1}{8}$in) thick. To make the trousers, cut two 6.5 × 5cm (2½ × 2in) rectangles and wrap them around the legs, securing them with a little water at the back.
3 Make a fairly portly oval of dough for the man's body and fix this on top of the legs. Do not be too concerned about the join as it will not show. Cut out a 6.5cm (2½in) square of dough and cut this diagonally into two triangles. Wrap one of these triangles around the right-hand side (*his* right side) of the man's chest so that the cut edge runs across him. Overlapping the first triangle slightly, cover his left side in the same way. Before securing this piece, trim off the point of the triangle where it crosses over to shape the coat front.

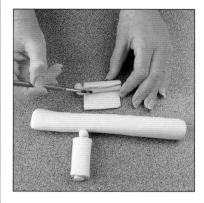

Wrapping the trousers around the legs.

4 Cut a pear-shaped piece of dough, about 4.5cm (1¾in) across the fattest part and 6.5cm (2½in) high. Cut a deep notch in the broad end so that it looks a little like a heart shape and fix this upside down on the figure's back to make coat-tails. Eventually, his right-hand coat-tail will not show because of the female figure but make sure that the left tail is pulled slightly to the side so that it will show from the front.

5 Attach the man to the base rope about 2.5cm (1in) from the right side. Cut two small, tapering strips of dough for coat lapels and secure them in place. Make buttons for the front of the coat from four tiny balls of flattened dough.

6 Make a pair of arms and hands, see page 13, and wrap two thin ropes of dough around these to make cuffs. Attach the arms to the body at the shoulders but leave the hands free. Make a small carol sheet out of a thin piece of dough, about 4 × 2.5cm (1½ × 1in). Roll up one end to make a scroll, then arrange it in the hands so that it looks as if the man is holding it.

7 Make a ball of dough for his head. Mark eyes and an open, singing, mouth with a cocktail stick (toothpick). Make a nose from a small ball of dough. Use the 2.5cm (1in) round cutter to cut out the brim of the hat. Squeeze its edges between your thumb and forefinger to make them thin and to slightly enlarge the brim.

8 Make a short cylinder of dough for the crown of the hat and score it with the back of a knife to make it look slightly battered. Fit the crown on the brim, then put the hat on his head at a slight angle. Push a small amount of dough through the sieve and arrange it in little patches, sticking out from under the hat and on the cheeks to make hair and sideburns.

9 Cut two thin strips of dough 7cm × 12mm (2¾ × ½in). Press the strips gently against the finest strip cutter so that they are indented along their length to look like ribbed knitting. Cross these strips across the man's chest and around his neck to make a scarf. Push some dough through the garlic press to make a fringe for the scarf, see page 12.

10 Make the lady a slightly thinner set of legs and feet, measuring 6.5cm (2½in) long and lay them on the work surface. Make a far slimmer oval of dough for her body and fix it to her legs. Cut a fluted circle of thinly rolled dough and frill the edges with a cocktail stick (toothpick), see page 14. Remove the centre of the circle with the 2.5cm (1in) round cutter, then cut the remaining frilled ring to make a strip. Fit this around the lady's legs, just above her ankles, to represent the edge of her petticoat.

11 Cut a 16.5 × 5cm (6½ × 2in) rectangle of thinly rolled-out dough and lay it vertically on the surface. Dampen a point in the middle of the top edge of the dough. Fold about 2.5cm (1in) of dough inwards on each side of the damp spot, making an inverted pleat. Dust some flour over the top of this pleat to take up any spare moisture and then roll the top 6mm (¼in) of it with a rolling pin to secure it in place. Trim the top edge straight again and trim the side edges of the rectangle at a slant, so that the top is slightly narrower than the bottom.

12 Fit the pleated skirt around the lady's waist and fold the edges underneath her body and petticoat. The bottom of the skirt should cover the top edge of the frill to conceal the fact that there is no petticoat. Arrange the hemline of the skirt so that the petticoat frill shows a little and she looks quite windblown. There is no need to conceal the top edge of the skirt as it will not show.

13 Make two arms and a scroll of carols and fit these in a similar way to the man's arms. Make the lady a little round head and mark the

Carol Singers

features as before but give her a smaller nose; do not add the hair and hat yet.

14 Cut a triangle of thinly rolled dough, 10cm (4in) across the base and with 11.5cm (4½in) sides. Drape this around the lady's shoulders like a shawl. Cross over the front corners of the shawl. Flatten a small oval of dough and attach it where she might have a brooch to hold the shawl in place. Make some thick fringing for the shawl with short lengths of dough from the garlic press.

15 Cut out a 5cm (2in) circle of rolled-out dough and cut it in half. Fit one half over the back of her head to represent the back of her bonnet, then fit the other half so that it over-laps the first slightly and comes forward to form a peak. Shape the second half by pressing the dough lightly between your thumb and forefinger. Decorate the join with a row of small flowers made using a blossom plunger cutter.

16 Attach a few short strands of dough extruding through the garlic press on either side of her face to represent ringlets. Cut four very thin strips of dough with the fine strip cutter to make ribbons for her bonnet. Run one strip under her chin, then notch the ends of two more strips. Attach these to the first strip at one side of her face and let the notched ends hang down over her shawl. Make a bow with the third strip, see page 13, and fix this under her chin, over the ribbons.

17 To make the lamp-post make a 15cm (6in) long rope which is quite thick at one end and tapering to become pencil-thin at the other end. Wrap three thin ropes of dough around it at regular intervals by way of dec-oration. Fix the fatter end to the base to the left of the lady.

18 Lay another thin 2.5cm (1in) long rope across the top of the lamp-post. Stand two more equally thin, 12mm (½in) long ropes on either end of the first to produce a 'U' shape and top this off with the small, hand-modelled triangle of dough, about 4.5cm (1¾in) across the bottom and 1.5cm (¾in) on each side. Decorate the top of the triangle with two small balls of dough, the top being the smallest. Model a tiny flame and attach it to the middle of the lamp. Then use the retracted ballpoint pen to indent the bottoms of the triangle and the lamp, and the three decorative ropes.

19 Cover the base with several flattened balls of dough, packed tightly together to represent cobblestones.

20 Make two dog's legs by rolling two very thin ropes about 2.5cm (1in) long. Set these aside for a moment and model a haunch with a leg attached by rolling a 2.5cm (1in) long rope the same thickness as the first pair of legs at one end but growing thicker towards the other end. Flatten the thick end slightly to represent the haunch. Make three short cuts in the bottom of each leg to represent paws.

21 Model an oval of dough for the dog's body and lean this at a slight angle against the male figure's left leg. Fit the two front legs to the front of the body and the haunch and leg to the back, so that the dog appears to be sitting down. Model a smaller oval of dough for the head and fix this onto the dog, tipped up in the direction of the man's face. Mark two eyes and an open mouth with a cocktail stick (toothpick) so that the dog appears to be howling and joining in with the singing. Cut two triangular ears and fit these well back on the dog's head to accentuate the angle of the head. Make a 2.5cm (1in) long tapering rope and fit this on the dog for a tail. Finally, add a small triangular knob of dough just above the mouth for his nose and score the whole dog with your cocktail stick to simulate fur.

22 Push a hanging hook into each end of the

base and one into the female figure's hat. Bake at 145°C (290°F/Gas 1½) for about 3 hours.

Painting and Finishing

● Mix some flesh colour, see page 42, and paint the faces of the figures. Use Yellow Ochre to paint the man's trousers and while this is drying paint his jacket with Fir Green. When both jacket and trousers are dry, paint his scarf and gloves in pure Cadmium Red. Then use a fine brush or preferably a rigger and the same colour to paint the red checks on his trousers. When this is dry use some Fir Green to paint a finer check between the red lines, see page 112. Use Jet black to paint the man's lapels, buttons, hat, boots and cuffs.

Paint the lady's shawl in a mixture of white and Ultramarine. While this is drying, paint her skirt pure Magenta and then use the same colour to paint a fine check on her shawl. Allow this to dry thoroughly. Using Ultramarine and white again, mix a slightly darker blue to paint another check between the first lines on the shawl.

Paint the bonnet, ribbons and gloves in pure Spectrum Violet and the flowers on the bonnet with a selection of pale Violets and Magentas, made by mixing white with both these colours.

When the dress is completely dry, paint a triangular pattern all over it in white, using three small dots. While you still have the white on your brush, make it a little more watery and paint both the scrolls and her petticoat and cuffs. When the scrolls are dry, make a few uneven black lines on them to represent writing and paint her boots and the markings on his gloves black.

To finish the lady, paint a miniature portrait on her brooch. Alternatively, paint two or three simple flowers or just paint it black, like ebony.

Paint the dog mainly Burnt Sienna, just dabbing a little white on his chest, tail and paws when the base is dry. Paint his nose and eyes black, putting a little crescent of white at the bottom of his eye when the black is dry, to give the impression that he is looking up. Mix some pink from Cadmium Red and white, and paint the inside of the dog's mouth.

Make up watery Olive Green to paint the lamp post; leave to dry. Paint the balls at the top and the decorative indentations in Gold. If you painted an elaborate brooch, you could also give it a gold frame.

Mix bright orange using Cadmium Red and Yellow for the flame, and add a dab of pure Cadmium Yellow while the paint is still wet.

Mix some white and black together in rather a watery consistency and paint this onto the cobbles. While the paint is still wet, add some watery dabs of blues, violets and pinks to give it some life – but take care not to overdo this effect.

These little figures are made with small gingerbread cutters. They may be used as brooches or refrigerator magnets.

71

HOUSES AND COTTAGES

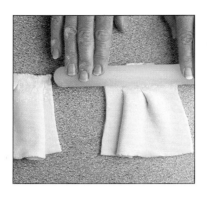

Nursery Window
Make sure that all the pleats are facing towards the middle before rolling the top edge flat.

Dough houses make wonderful house-warming presents, especially if you can actually reproduce the new home. This section also covers windows and furniture for your houses.

·NURSERY WINDOW·

Window Template, see page 138
thin card
$\frac{3}{4}$ quantity Paste Dough, see page 10
small heart cutter
old retractable ballpoint pen
modelling tool
floristry wire
Hanging Hooks, see page 17

1 Trace the template, see page 138, then cut it out in thin card. Roll out one-third of the dough to 6mm ($\frac{1}{4}$in) thick, then cut a rectangle of dough measuring 14 × 10cm ($5\frac{1}{2}$ × 4in) and place it on a baking sheet. Use the window template to impress the shape of the panes in the dough. Press it down firmly, then lift it off cleanly each time. Use a sharp knife to cut around the indentations. Carefully remove the squares of dough.

2 Make a rope of dough, a little fatter than a finger and 14cm ($5\frac{1}{4}$in) long, and flatten it slightly. Dampen the rope and butt it up to the dough under one long edge of the window to form the sill. Decorate the sill with heart indentations, made by gently pressing the cutter into the dough, and dots made with the pen.

3 Take a generous two-thirds of the remaining dough and roll out thinly. Cut out two curtains (drapes), measuring 15 × 12.5cm (6 × 5in) and one pelmet (valance) measuring 30 × 4cm (12 × $1\frac{1}{2}$in). Pleat each curtain along the top, dampening the pleats to hold them in place and making sure that, on each curtain, they face the middle of the window when in position. Dust the pleats with a little flour, if necessary, to absorb any excess moisture, then carefully roll out their top edge so that they are not too bulky.

4 Wet the top and side edges of the window and fix the curtains (drapes) in place, arranging them as though they are blowing in a breeze. Remember to leave enough room for the bear and the flowers on the window sill. Trim off any excess dough at the top before pleating and fitting the pelmet (valance) using the same technique.

5 Make a teddy bear, see page 15, and place him on the window sill with one paw extended to hold a honey jar. Follow the instructions for making pots, step 5, page 75, to make the honey jar. Make the large flower vase by the same method; however, instead of indenting a rim, remove the pot from the modelling tool and carefully mould it into a vase shape by pressing and curving the rim outwards with your fingers.

6 Place the vase on the window sill, then cut out and arrange some leaves in it. Take several small balls of dough and model them into ovals, then flatten them slightly at one end so that they resemble tulips. Cut a short piece

Nursery Window

Cat Napping
*Cutting the scalloped edge for the
blind (shade).*

of floristry wire, dampen one end and push it into a tulip. Repeat with the remaining flowers, then arrange them in the pot among the leaves.

7 Attach a hanging hook at either end of the top of the window and bake at 145°C (290°F/ Gas 1½) for about 2½ hours.

Painting and Finishing

● The curtains (drapes) are painted with a mixture of Ultramarine and Permanent White. When dry the stripes are painted in Permanent White, with a steady hand!

The bear is painted with Yellow Ochre, with just a blush of watery Red Ochre on his nose and whisker pads.

The pot is also painted in watery Red Ochre and decorated, when dry, with Gold. The bear's bow, hearts and some of the tulips are painted in various combinations of Magenta and white, while other tulips are painted with Spectrum Violet. The leaves are painted in Olive Green and the honey pot is pale pink with black lettering.

·CAT NAPPING·

Window Template, see page 138
thin card
¼ quantity Paste Dough, see page 10
small heart cutter
cocktail stick (toothpick)
modelling tool
small bird cutter
small leaf cutter
blossom plunger cutter
floristry wire
small rose cutter

1 Trace the window template, see page 138, then cut it out in thin card. Roll out half the dough to approximately 6mm (¼ in) thick. Cut out a rectangle measuring 12.5 × 9cm (5 × 3½in), place it on a baking sheet and press the window template down on the dough. Lift off the template to leave the imprint and repeat for all six panes, arranged in pairs. Cut around each imprint and carefully remove the squares of dough.

2 Roll out some dough slightly thinner than above and cut out a rectangle 9 × 6.5cm (3½ × 2½in). Using a sharp knife, carefully scallop one of the longer edges for the bottom edge of the blind (shade). Dampen the plain sides of the dough and fix it in place behind the window frame so that the scalloped edge reaches halfway down. Use the heart cutter and cocktail stick (toothpick) to mark a pattern of hearts and dots on the blind (shade).

3 Roll a small piece of dough into a rope, as thick as a finger and approximately 15cm (6in) long, see page 11. Wet both ends of this and fix it in the shape of an arch across the top of the window. Mould another small rope into a circle to fill the space between the top of the window and the arch. Fix two small balls of dough where the arch joins the window and one where the arch joins the circle. Indent the balls with the end of the modelling tool and decorate the circle in the same way. Roll out a small piece of dough, cut out a bird and fix it in place where the window joins the circle.

4 Make a slightly thicker rope than that used for the arch and flatten it slightly. Wet the top of the dough rope and butt it firmly up against the bottom of the window to make a sill.

5 Mould a small ball of dough into a flower pot, then carefully push the rounded end of the modelling tool in it to hollow it out. While the dough is still on the modelling tool, use the back of a knife to make a slight indentation around the top to form a rim. Carefully remove the modelling tool and make two more pots. Wet the bottom of the pots and arrange them on the window sill.

6 Cut out several leaves and small blossoms from some thinly rolled dough. Mark veins on the leaves using the back of a knife, then arrange them in the pots. Push a short length of curved wire into each pot to represent a stalk. Push the free ends of the wires back against the window frame or against a leaf so that you have a firm base on which to attach the blossom. Form the flower heads at the top of the wires by fixing several small blossoms in a group.

7 Make a small sitting cat, see page 14, and place it on the window sill close to the pots. Fix the hanging hook and bake at 145°C (290°F / Gas 1½) for about 2 hours.

Painting and Finishing

● Slightly tint some watery Permanent White with a little Alizarin Crimson and paint the blind. While still damp, fill in the hearts with a slightly stronger mix of Alizarin and white. When dry, add the pale blue dots and border made from Ultramarine and white.

Using pure Sap Green, paint the windowsill and the circles on the arch. Add a little Red Ochre to this mix to make a darker green for the leaves. Paint the pots with fairly watery Red Ochre and the cat with Lamp Black and white. The little bird should also be painted white and decorated with a little pink chest and pale blue wings. The cat's ear linings and whisker pads are painted in the same pink, and his bow is pale blue with white dots. The flowers are Spectrum Red.

CRAFT TIP

Cocktail sticks (toothpicks), which are often used for dough modelling, are sometimes sold in square-topped plastic pots. These pots make wonderful window cutters when empty.

·ROSE COTTAGE·

Cottage Template, see page 138
Window Template, see page 138
thin card
¾ quantity Paste Dough, see page 10
heart cutters
rose cutters
primrose cutter
clay gun
retractable ballpoint pen
blossom plunger cutter

1   Trace the templates, then cut them out in thin card. Roll out half the dough to 6mm ($\frac{1}{2}$in) thick. Press the cottage template on the dough so that it leaves an imprint when lifted, then cut around this and place the dough cottage on a baking sheet.

2   Use the window template in the same way, to make two upstairs windows and one downstairs window, making sure that you leave sufficient room for the shutters on either side of each window. Lift out the squares of dough from the centre of each window and cut each square in half to make shutters. Stamp out a heart shape in each half. Wet the backs of the shutters and fix them on either side of the windows. Indicate that the shutters are slatted by indenting them vertically with the back of a knife.

3   Roll out some dough thinly and use the largest rose cutter to cut out about 30 circles. Dampen the roof area, then overlap the circles in three rows to represent tiles, starting with the bottom row. Dampen the circles as you place them on the cottage. Model a small piece of dough into a 4cm × 12mm (1$\frac{1}{2}$ × $\frac{1}{2}$in) oblong. Use the back of a knife to indent a rim at the top, then tuck this chimney behind the end tiles.

4   Cut out a triangle with 6.6cm (2$\frac{1}{2}$in)

sides. Use the primrose cutter to cut a flower shape from the middle of this, then fix it to the roof with the base level with the bottom row of tiles so that it looks like a gable. To decorate the edge of the gable and the ridge of the roof, use the clay gun fitted with the disc with the largest hole and extrude the dough in loops along the ridge and straight around the gable. Finish by indenting the edging with the point of the old pen.

5   Using the back of a knife, indent a slatted door measuring 5 × 3cm (2 × 1$\frac{1}{2}$in) in the dough next to the downstairs window. Finish the door with a tiny ball of dough for a handle. To make the porch, cut a triangle with 4cm (1$\frac{1}{2}$in) sides. Fix this in position over the door, wedging a small ball of dough underneath it to make it bulge out slightly. Using the smallest rose cutter, cut out eleven circles and arrange ten of these overlapping on the porch for tiles. Place the extra circle beside the door for the house number.

6   Make a 15cm (6in) rope, slightly fatter than a finger, see page 11, and butt this up against the bottom of the cottage, flattening it out slightly at the same time. Place a small ball of dough on one end of the rope to represent a tub. Cut six 1.5cm × 6mm ($\frac{3}{4}$ × $\frac{1}{4}$in) strips of rolled-out dough and fix them vertically on the ball of dough to form the panels. Flatten a thin rope of dough to make the band around the tub and mark nails in it using the point of an old pen.

7   Roll an irregular rope of dough which tapers out at one end and arrange it so that the thick end appears to be growing out of the tub and the tapered end drapes over the porch. Cut some tiny leaves, freehand, out of thinly rolled dough and arrange them along the length of the rose tree. Make several small rosebuds, see page 15, and dot these among the leaves.

Rose Cottage

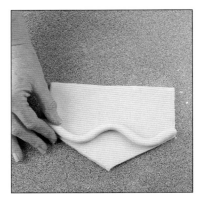

House with a Georgian Door
Putting on one of the gables.

I made this house after a trip to Dublin, a city of buildings with blue plaques and the most wonderful Georgian doors. Unfortunately, that idea seems to have got mixed up with a Hansel and Gretel cottage, which I have had my eye on for years. Dough architects are allowed such licence . . . and the woman in the window seems to be quite happy.

8 Make a cat, see page 14, to sit in front of the door. Fit the sieve-like disc in the clay gun and extrude some fine strands of dough. Fix these along the front of the cottage for grass and stems in a flower border. Arrange small blossoms among the grass. The hollyhock, at the side of the cottage, is made by building up a spike of tiny balls of dough and indenting each with the point of the pen.

9 Push a hanging hook into either side of the roof and bake at 145°C (290°F/Gas 1½) for 2½ hours.

Painting and Finishing

● Wash some very watery Red Ochre over the tiles of the roof and porch. While still wet, blend patches of Olive Green on the tiles. Use the same green to paint the tub, then mix it a little thicker to paint the grass and leaves.

Mix some Ultramarine and white to paint the shutters, the edge of the flower-shaped window and the house number plate. Use a mixture of Red Orchre and Yellow Ochre for the cat, adding some white markings. Paint his eyes, the door knob and the rim around the tub with Lamp Black.

Mix a little Rose Madder and white to paint the roses and some of the other flowers. Finish the flowers in various mixtures of reds, pinks and white. Finally, paint in the house number in black. Add a little Red Ochre to the black to paint the earth in the tub and the trunk of the rose tree.

· HOUSE WITH A · GEORGIAN DOOR

1¼ quantities Basic Dough, see page 10
plastic ruler
2.5cm (1in) square cutter
retracted ballpoint pen
2.5cm (1in) and 12mm (½in) round cutters
small leaf cutter
small blossom plunger cutter
clay gun
large tulip-shaped stamens
cocktail stick (toothpick)
2 Hanging Hooks, see page 17
1 hairpin

1 Roll out half the dough to 6mm (¼in) thick. Using a well-floured plastic ruler and a sharp knife, cut out a 17.5 × 15cm (7 × 6in) rectangle. Lay this horizontally on the work surface, then mark the centre of the top edge and mark both sides, 5cm (2in) from the top. Lay the ruler between the centre mark and one of the side marks, then cut off and discard a triangle of dough. Do the same on the other side to make a rudimentary house shape. Lay this on a baking tray.

2 Take a handful of dough and make a 22.5cm (9in) long finger-thick rope. Starting at the point where the roof begins to slope, curve the rope of dough up and down across the width of the house so that it forms the shape of two gables. Decorate the rope with the retracted ballpoint pen.

3 Make a second rope of the same size as the last one and flatten this slightly with your fingertips before laying it on its side and pushing it up against the base of the house. Secure it in position with a little water.

4 To make the steps, prepare three pencil-

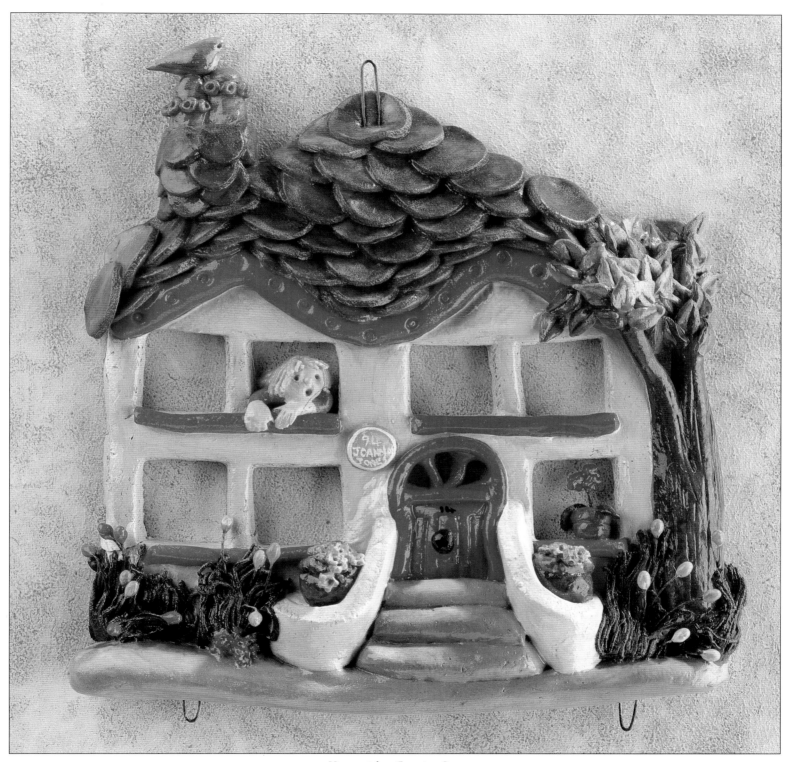

House with a Georgian Door

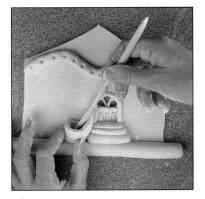

Fixing a balustrade.

DOUGH HOUSES

Although making house portraits is not as difficult as it might sound, features like balconies and fire escapes can tax your ingenuity.

The alternative to actually copying a house is to allow your imagination to take over and invent the fantasy home of your dreams. Then you can really let yourself go, giving it every architectual feature you have ever coveted . . . after all it might be as close as you'll ever get to owning an ancestral home!

thick ropes, 6.5cm ($2\frac{1}{2}$in), 5cm (2in) and 4cm ($1\frac{1}{2}$in) in length. Flatten the ropes slightly with your fingers, then arrange the longest rope to form the bottom step, the middle-size rope above it and the shortest one at the top. Place these on the ledge at the base of the house so that the bottom step begins 9cm ($3\frac{1}{2}$in) from the left-hand side.

5 Make a very thin rope measuring about 10cm (4in) long. Loop this in the shape of an arched doorway, starting and finishing on either side of the top step. Use the small leaf cutter to cut out three shapes in the door symmetrically placed in the position of a fan light. Then place another very thin rope across the door just underneath the fan light. Use the back of a knife to indent panels in the lower half of the door and place a small ball of dough in the centre for a handle.

6 Cut out three sets of double windows with the square cutter: two on either side at the top of the house and one set to the left of the door. Place a single window to the right of the door. Take care when you are arranging the windows, to make them symmetrical and leave enough room on either side of the door for the balustrade. Make thin, flattened ropes of dough for windowsills on all the windows.

7 To make the balustrades, roll out some dough to 6mm ($\frac{1}{4}$in) thick and cut out two 10 × 2.5cm (4 × 1in) oblongs. Arrange these on either side of the steps, securing one end of each on the wall beside the top step and door. Lay the remaining lengths of each oblong along the steps until you get to the last 5cm (2in). Then sweep each one around into coils facing in opposite directions. Secure each coil to the ledge at the base of the house with a little water.

8 Knead any scraps of dough together with a little water and roll out to 3mm ($\frac{1}{8}$in) thick and cut out about fifty 2.5cm (1in) circles.

Starting along the gables, arrange these on the roof as tiles. Make a short cylinder of dough for the chimney stack and place it on one side of the roof. Cut out a few smaller tiles using a 12mm ($\frac{1}{2}$in) round cutter and place these around the chimney stack. Make two smaller cylinders for the chimney pots and secure them on top of the stack. Encircle both of these with little balls of dough, pricking each one in the middle with a cocktail stick (toothpick) to make them more ornamental. Then model a little pigeon to sit on the top, see page 15.

9 Make a 12.5cm (5in) long, thick rope of dough for the tree trunk. Split the top 6.5cm ($2\frac{1}{2}$in) in two, then split the two branches in two again to make more branches. Fix the tree in place against the right-hand side of the house and score the trunk with a knife to make it look more like wood. Cut out about 35 small leaves and arrange these at the top of the tree so that they cover part of the branches and some of the roof.

10 Arrange some clay-gun grass at the bottom of the tree and along the border on the left-hand side of the ledge.

11 To make a flower pot, make a ball of dough, then hollow it out a little with the round end of a modelling tool. Hold the dough on the modelling tool while you run the back of your knife around it, a little way in from the edge, to make a lip. Make two matching pots and fix them onto the coiled parts of the balustrade. Make a smaller one to go in the right-hand single window.

12 Cut out a small leaf and split it length-ways in two to make two leaves for the smaller pot. Secure these in place so that they are leaning over the edge a little, then stick the stem of one of the tulip stamens into the centre of the pot. Cut out about 30 little blossoms and arrange three of these at the top of the stem. Use the others to fill the

balustrade pots and to make a little cluster of polyanthus at the base of the left-hand clumps of grass.

13 Cut about ten of the tulip stamens in half and stick them in among the grass on either side of the steps. Model a couple of tiny arms and hands, see page 13, and lay these over the window sill of the left-hand top window. Then make a little head with some clay gun hair and rest it on top of one of the arms. Cut out a 12mm ($\frac{1}{2}$in) circle and place it on the wall in the middle of the house.

14 As the house is heavy, push one hairpin through the top of the roof, just leaving the top from which to hang the plaque and place two hanging hooks under the ledge for fixing pins. Bake the house at 145°C (290°F/Gas 1$\frac{1}{2}$) for about 2$\frac{1}{2}$ hours.

Painting and Finishing

● Mix very watery white and add a touch of Raw Umber to give it a light beige appearance. Paint this on the house walls and balustrades. Add a spot of Jet black and paint the steps and the ledge. Use pure Flame Red to paint the gables, windowsills and door, adding a black knob when dry.

Add a touch of Red Ochre to Burnt Sienna for the tiles and flowerpots, but add quite a lot of water to this when painting tiles.

Paint the grass in pure Olive Green and add varying amounts of yellow and white to paint leaves on the tree. Paint the tree trunk in pure Burnt Sienna. Use pure Magenta for some of the tulips and the polyanthus. Add a little white to this for the flowers in the large pots. Use the colours you used for the tree leaves to paint a few free-hand leaves around the potted flowers. Make some of the tulips pink (white added to Flame Red), then paint the rest pure Cadmium Yellow.

Dull some Flame Red with a little Raw Umber to paint the flowers in the window. Give all the small flowers yellow centres.

Paint the pigeon with the same colour used on the front steps, blending some Magenta into the feathers and even add a little green. While you have diluted Magenta on your brush, paint sleeves on the figure in the window. Mix up flesh colour, see page 42, to paint her face and hands.

Mix some pale blue and paint the plaque. You could paint the owner's name and date of moving on the plaque in white. Remember to paint a white circle around the edge to make it look authentic.

·TOWN HOUSE·

This house is full of my unfulfilled fantasies – I have longed for a house with a green-tiled roof ever since I was a child, and I am still trying to grow a wisteria long enough for it to cascade down the walls of my house. I would also love a balcony; and my Austrian blinds remain stubbornly at the planning stage . . . even the ginger cat is a long-held ambition and although I have got one who visits, he isn't really mine – yet!

$\frac{3}{4}$ quantity Basic Dough, see page 10
plastic ruler
2.5cm (1in) square cutter
2.5cm (1in) and 12mm ($\frac{1}{2}$in) round cutters
retracted ballpoint pen
cocktail stick (toothpick)
thin plastic drinking straw
small leaf cutter
small blossom plunger cutter
2 Hanging Hooks, see page 17

1 Take half of the dough and roll it out to 6mm ($\frac{1}{2}$in) thick. Using a well-floured ruler and a sharp knife, cut out a 16.5 × 9cm (6$\frac{1}{2}$ × 3$\frac{1}{2}$in) rectangle of dough. Lay this vertically on

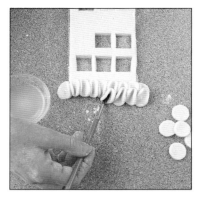

Fixing on the roof tiles.

a baking tray and use the square cutter to cut out three evenly spaced windows about 2.5cm (1in) from the top.

2 Leaving a space of about 12mm ($\frac{1}{2}$in), cut a further two squares below the left-hand windows. Cut one more window in the right-hand corner, 12mm ($\frac{1}{2}$in) from the bottom.

3 Take a sharp knife with a good point and use the back of the blade to indent the shape of a front door to the left of the lower window. The door should be 4 × 2cm ($1\frac{1}{2}$ × $\frac{3}{4}$in).

4 Use the same technique to mark a 4 × 2.5cm ($1\frac{1}{2}$ × 1in) garage door to the left of the front door. Cut out two small windows in the top of the front door and use the back of the knife to indent panels at the bottom. Mark the garage door in the same way, with panelled double doors each with two windows. Make three small balls of dough for knobs; place one on the front door and two on the garage.

5 Roll a 4cm ($1\frac{1}{2}$in) long finger-thick rope of dough and flatten it to make a door step. Secure this in position by the front door. Model two tiny milk bottle shapes to stand on the door step. Cut a thin strip of rolled-out dough about 11.5cm × 6mm ($4\frac{1}{2}$ × $\frac{1}{4}$in) and attach it under the top set of windows.

6 Roll out some dough to 3mm ($\frac{1}{8}$in) thick and cut out 35, 2.5cm (1in) circles. Fix about ten of these to the top of the house, curving them towards each other sideways so that they do not lie flat. Fix a second, slightly shorter, line of tiles on top of these, allowing the second row to half cover the first. Arrange a third and fourth row in the same way, making each one shorter than the one before. Finish the top of the roof with an ornamental ridge made from a thin rope of dough, about 7.5cm (3in) long. Indent this with the retracted ballpoint pen and decorate the top with a row of little dough balls.

7 Cut out 16, 12mm ($\frac{1}{2}$in) circles and make similar roofs for the front door and garage. These should be only two-tiles high and finished with a tiny rope indented with the cocktail stick (toothpick).

8 To make the balcony, roll out some dough to 6mm ($\frac{1}{4}$in) thick and cut out a 12mm × 8cm ($\frac{1}{2}$ × $3\frac{1}{4}$in) rectangle. Attach this, edge on, under the double window. Cut ten 2.5cm (1in) lengths from the drinking straws and carefully stick these into the rectangle, around the edge, to represent the railings of the balcony. Make a pencil-thin, 12cm ($4\frac{3}{4}$in) long, rope and lay it carefully on the tops of the drinking straws. Attach both ends of this rope to the wall and press down very gently so that the straws become slightly embedded. Decorate it with the retracted ballpoint pen.

9 To make the wisteria tree, prepare two thin, tapering ropes, about 20cm (8in) long. Twist the first 7.5cm (3in) of the fatter ends together. Secure the twisted end of the ropes against the right-hand side of the house with a little water and allow the two tapering ends to drape over and under the balcony.

10 Cut about 18 leaves from some thinly rolled dough and indent a vein down the middle of each with the back of a knife. Attach these on the wisteria tree, mainly on the single ropes, at irregular intervals. Make several tiny balls of dough and secure them onto the tree in drooping bunches. Indent the centre of each ball with a cocktail stick (toothpick) to ensure that they do not look like grapes.

11 For the Austrian blinds, cut out three 3cm ($1\frac{1}{2}$in) squares of thinly rolled dough. Take one of these and use the cocktail stick (toothpick) like a miniature rolling pin to roll it out a little more. Still using the cocktail stick, push the thinned dough up into folds and catch these together on either side of the square to make an Austrian blind. Do the same with the two other squares. Fit the blinds into the top three windows.

12 To make the blind in the bottom window, cut a rectangle 4cm × 12mm (1½ × ½in). Cut a zig-zag border along one of the long edges using the point of a sharp knife. Wet the other edges slightly. With the decorated border downwards, carefully slide this piece of dough under the house and fit it into position behind the window. Make a row of holes just above the edge with the cocktail stick.

13 Make a tiny cat, see page 14, to sit on the windowsill. Put two hanging hooks in either end of the roof and bake the house at 145°C (290°F/gas 1½) for about 1½ hours.

Painting and Finishing

● Add a spot of Ultramarine to some really watery white, and paint the house walls and windowsills with this pale blue mixture. Add a little Jet Black to what is left and wash this over the door step and the balcony floor.

Dilute some Viridian and mix in a touch of Jet Black before painting all the tiles with this colour. Then paint the roof ridges in pure Burnt Sienna and the doors and the balcony in pure Olive Green.

Dilute the remains of the Olive Green and add the smallest touch of Burnt Sienna to get the colour for the wisteria leaves. To get a sort of smudgy, purple-brown for the trunk and branches of the tree, add a touch more brown and a spot of Spectrum Violet to the leaf mixture. Paint this on in a very watery way and allow it to dry before adding the pinks and violets of the flowers.

Make a variety of colours for the flowers by playing with Spectrum Violet, Alizarin Crimson, Permanent White and Ultramarine. When they are dry, give each of the flowers a dab of Cadmium Yellow in the centre.

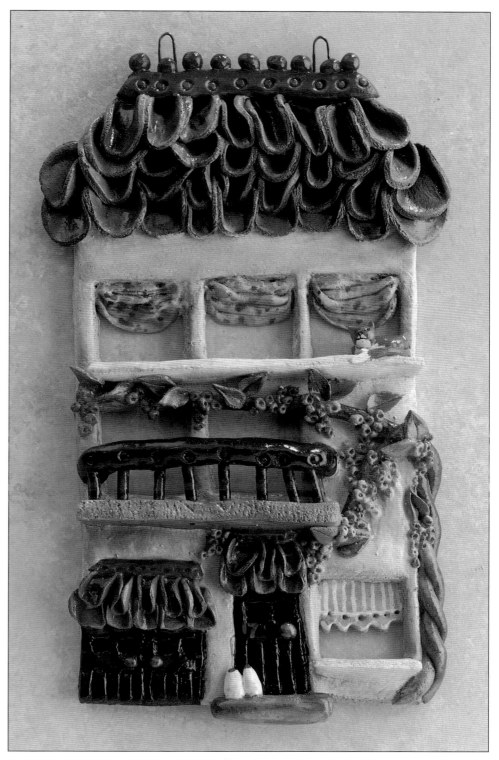

Town House

Mix some Alizarin Crimson and white together to get the colour of the downstairs blind and when this is dry paint white stripes and a border on it.

Mix Cadmium Red and Cadmium Yellow together to make the colour for the cat. Paint some white patches on his face, chest and paws and leave to dry. Then paint his eyes, nose and mouth with black. You will probably find enough bright colours on your palette to smudge onto the Austrian blinds and enough white to paint the milk bottles. Finally, paint the door knobs and the number in gold.

·KITCHEN DRESSER·

Once you have modelled a house, have a go at this dresser for the kitchen.

$\frac{1}{2}$ quantity Paste Dough, see page 10
small heart cutter
modelling tool · rose cutters
4 cloves · small leaf cutter
floristry wire · daisy cutter
2 Hanging Hooks, see page 17

1 Roll out one-third of the dough to 9mm ($\frac{3}{8}$in) thick. Cut a rectangle measuring 14 × 9cm ($5\frac{1}{2}$ × $3\frac{1}{2}$in) and lay it on a baking sheet. Roll some more dough to 6mm ($\frac{1}{4}$in) thick and cut out a smaller rectangle measuring 9 × 4cm ($3\frac{1}{2}$ × $1\frac{1}{2}$in).

2 Dampen the back of the smaller dough rectangle and lay it across the bottom of the first rectangle in position for the drawers. Use the back of a knife to indent the outline of drawers fairly deeply, then decorate them by indenting them with the small heart cutter. Fix a small ball of dough on each for a handle.

3 Roll out some more dough to 6mm ($\frac{1}{4}$in) thick and cut out three shelves measuring 7.5cm × 6mm (3 × $\frac{1}{4}$in). Cut two 10cm × 9mm (4 × $\frac{3}{8}$in) strips, one 9cm × 12mm ($3\frac{1}{2}$ × $\frac{1}{2}$in) strip and one 9 × 1.5cm ($3\frac{1}{2}$ × $\frac{3}{4}$in) strip. Arrange the three shelves evenly along the back of the dresser so that the bottom shelf is 2.5cm (1in) above the drawers and the top one is a similar distance below the dresser top.

4 Fix the pair of cut strips vertically along the sides of the shelves. Make several small, decorative indentations along the edges of these strips with a modelling tool.

5 Fix the 1.5cm ($\frac{3}{4}$in) wide strip across the top of the dresser, parallel with the shelves. Cut three heart shapes evenly across the remaining strip and mark it with decorative indentations as before. Fix this across the top of the dresser. Place two small balls of dough at the bottom of the dresser for feet.

6 To make the plates, use the medium rose cutter to cut five circles of dough. Press the middles in slightly with your finger. Arrange one plate on the bottom shelf and four on the next one up. Make four saucers in the same way using the smallest rose cutter. Place these on the shelf above the plates.

7 Discard the star-shaped ends off four cloves, then push the remaining stalks a little way into the edge of the top shelf to represent hooks. Make four very fine ropes of dough each about 12mm ($\frac{1}{2}$in) long and curve one of these over each of the clove stalks to represent cup handles. Make the cups by using the rounded end of the modelling tool to hollow out four small balls of dough. Dampen the outsides of the cups and carefully butt them up to the handles.

8 Make three bowls of different sizes as for the cups. Place the largest on top of the dresser, the smallest on the top shelf and the medium bowl on the bottom shelf, next to the single plate.

9 Make a cat, see page 14, and sit him next

Kitchen Dresser

to the medium bowl. Fill this bowl with little balls of dough to represent oranges.

10 Roll out some dough thinly and cut out several small leaves. Arrange these in the bowl on top of the dresser and push a 4cm (1½in) length of bent floristry wire into the centre. Cut out a daisy and attach this to the end of the wire with a dab of water. Arrange a small ball of dough in the centre of the daisy.

11 Fix two hanging hooks in either side of the top of the dresser and bake at 145°C (290°F/Gas 1½) for about 3 hours.

Painting and Finishing

● Mix a little Yellow Ochre into Olive Green and water it down quite a bit to get just the right colour for this old dresser. The hearts and the lining on the dresser are painted Red Ochre dulled with just a touch of Olive Green.

All the china is painted with Permanent White and decorated with a pale blue rim made from Ultramarine and white. The roses are painted with a mixture of Rose Malmaison and white and the leaves on the plates, and in the big bowl, are painted with Olive Green.

The oranges and the daisy are both painted with a mixture of Golden Yellow and Rose Malmaison. Use some Lamp Black and Permanent White on the cat, with just a little blush of watery Rose Malmaison in his ears and on his whisker pads.

DECORATED INITIALS

Decorated dough initials are quite definitely the most popular and acceptable of all the gift ideas in this book. I am sure that this is because everyone, no matter of what age, loves to be given something which has obviously been made especially for them. This is particularly true if the initial is made even more personal by the addition of some detail which is meaningful to the person for whom it is intended.

I have chosen three basic designs which are suitable for any age group, bearing in mind that the figures can be adapted to more adult interpretation if necessary. Most initials should measure at least 15cm (6in) high to allow plenty of room for a figure; however, those with a floral decoration may be made a little smaller if you wish.

TWISTED FLORAL ·INITIAL·

$\frac{3}{4}$ *quantity Basic Dough, see page 10*
leaf cutters
primrose cutters
blossom plunger cutter
rose cutters • carnation cutters
small heart cutter
Hanging Hook, see page 17

1   You will need to make twists of various lengths, depending on the letter required. Some people have difficulty working freehand, in which case it is easier to roughly sketch the shape of the letter in pencil on a baking sheet to use as a guide for shaping the dough twist.

2   Deciding on the technique for shaping the angles, such as the point at the bottom of a 'V', can be a problem. With twisted dough, it is generally more successful to curve the dough, rather than cutting and mitring it, which looks best with the rope-type initial. This is illustrated in the top of the 'A', see page 89, but be careful not to make the curve too broad when shaping 'V' as it can result in 'U'.

3   When you have moulded the basic letter to your satisfaction, roll out some dough and cut out some leaves. Mark veins on the leaves using the back of a knife and fix them over any joins in the dough initials, such as where the bar is attached across an 'A'.

4   Roll out more dough and cut out a selection of flowers: primroses, blossom, roses and carnations. Make the roses and carnations in various sizes, see pages 15 and 16. Arrange the flowers over the leaves. Roll out a small piece of dough and make a butterfly, see page 14. Attach the butterfly to the initial to balance the design. If you find that the butterfly's wings droop, then carefully prop them up with two small rolls of foil which can be removed after baking.

5   Fix a hanging hook in position and bake at 145°C (290°F/Gas $1\frac{1}{2}$) for about $2\frac{1}{2}$ hours.

Painting and Finishing

●   Paint the leaves roughly in Olive Green, leaving some small uneven patches of unpainted dough on them. While the green is still wet, paint the patches with a fairly watery mixture of Rose Malmaison, so that it runs slightly into the green. This should give the warm tint of new rose leaves.

Paint the carnation white and while still damp tip the frilly edges of the petals with a little watery Rose Malmaison. Blend the pink into the white, using a clean slightly damp brush, working towards the flower centre. Paint the rose with Rose Malmaison.

Mix a little Ultramarine and white for the forget-me-knots. Add a little pink mixture while still wet and blend the colours so that the flowers are a mixture of pale blue, pink and lavender, where the other two colours meet. The butterfly has a brown body and antennae, made by mixing red, yellow and blue. Add yellow centres to the forget-me-knots and orange ones to the primroses. Mix Rose Malmaison and Lemon Yellow to make orange. Varnish the back and front, several times.

·CLOWN INITIAL·

Clowns are a particularly good choice of decoration for a difficult letter because you can bend them around in all sorts of peculiar poses and they still look realistic.

1 quantity Basic Dough, see page 10
equipment for the Victorian Girl omitting sieve,
see page 46
clay gun (optional)
blossom plunger cutter
cocktail stick (toothpick)
garlic press
fine floristry wire
primrose cutter
Hanging Hooks, see page 17

1   Follow the instructions for Initial with Figure, see page 90, to mould the chosen initial in ropes of dough.

2   For legs, make two pencil-thin ropes of dough, each 10cm (4in) long. Using your fingertip, gently flatten a 4cm (1½in) end in each rope to represent boots. Place the legs in position on the initial.

3   Mould a pair of arms and hands, making the hands a little larger than usual, see page 13. Fix these in position on the initial in relation to the legs. If your clown is going to hold flowers, make the stems from dough extruded through a clay gun and cut out the flowers using the smallest blossom cutter, then fix them under his hands.

4   For the clown's pantaloons, roll out some dough and cut out two rectangles measuring 6.5 × 4cm (2½ × 1½in). Trim one narrow end of each rectangle in a slight curve, then turn in a narrow hem of dough around the curve and along the long sides. Dampen the legs and lay the pantaloons over them, tucking them under the initial at the waist.

5   Measure the arms and make baggy sleeves as for pantaloons. If the clown's body is beside, or in front of, the initial, make a body following the instructions for Victorian Girl, see page 46. Measure the clown and cut out a romper-suit shape, then turn a narrow hem in the dough on all sides apart from the neck.

6   Make two pieces of frill, see page 14. Carefully dampen the unfrilled edge of each piece and lay one over the other, then fix in place at the clown's neck.

7   Mould a small ball of dough for the head, mark the eyes and mouth with a cocktail stick (toothpick), then make the nose a little larger than usual, see page 46. Fix in place on the frill. Press some dough through a garlic press to make hair. Make a hat as for Victorian Girl. Stick a short length of wire into the hat, then push the opposite end of the wire into the initial. Cut out a medium-sized blossom and

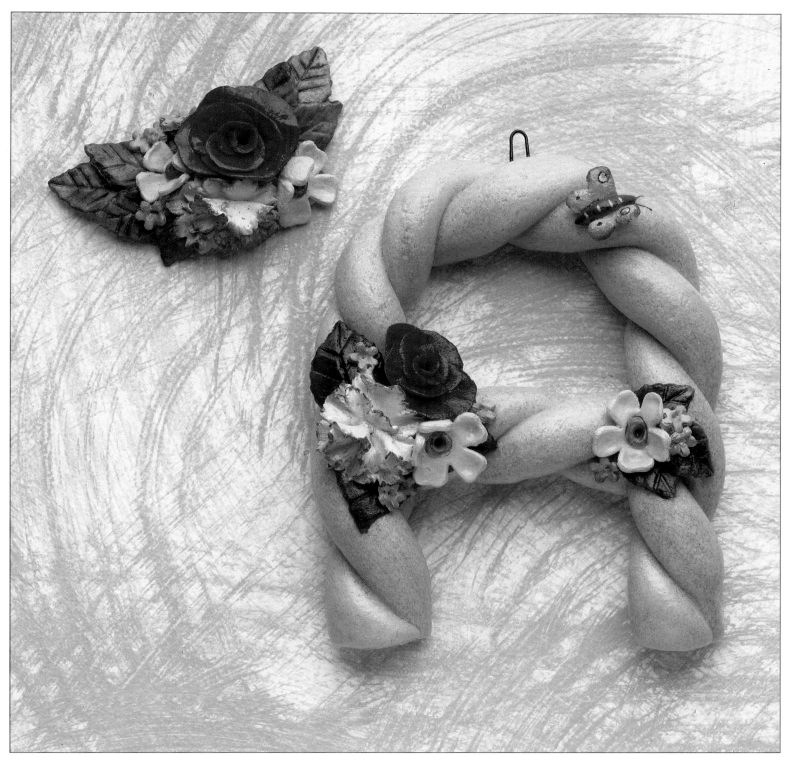

Twisted Floral Initial with a small nosegay of flowers

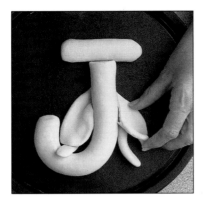

Clown Initial

*Arranging the clown's pantaloons
over his legs.*

Fixing flowers on the initial.

use to cover the end of the wire in the initial. Fix a small ball of dough in the middle of the flower.

8 Decorate any joins in the initial with flowers: I have used a primrose cutter to stamp out flowers but you might have other ideas. Fix hanging hooks in the dough and bake at 145°C (290°F/Gas 1½) for about 2½ hours.

Painting and Finishing

● Paint the face as for Victorian Girl, see page 48, omitting the eyes and mouth. When dry, carefully use pure Cadmium Red and a fine brush to paint a wide, curved clown's mouth and a big, fat nose. While this is drying, paint a white oval around one of the eyes and carefully outline the mouth in the same colour. When the white is dry, fill in both the eye holes in Lamp Black and paint a cross on the oval.

Using pure Magenta, paint the clown's suit and dry before painting large white spots. Continue the white on the gloves and the frill. Paint the shoes and hat with Lamp Black and the hair with a mixture of Cadmium Red and Cadmium Yellow.

Use a fine brush and gold to outline all the dots on the clown's suit. You may also edge the frill and make the eyelets for the shoe laces with gold.

Paint the flowers with different mixtures of Magenta and white, and Ultramarine and white. The hat, band, leaves and stems are painted in a mixture of Ultramarine, Cadmium Yellow and white. Finish off the shoelaces and the backs of the gloves in appropriate colours. Varnish, both back and front, several times.

·INITIAL WITH FIGURE·

Before you actually start modelling, it is a good idea to make a small sketch of the initial so that you can decide on the best position for the figure. Letters with bars and horizontal lines, such as A, H, B and P, generally look best with the figure arranged over the bar as illustrated, while letters like J, I and L usually look better with the figure leaning against the upright. There are rogue letters, such as K, W and N, but with a bit of jiggling about you will always find somewhere to fit the figure – so don't give up even if you have got a friend called Zaria!

1 quantity Basic Dough, see page 10
Victorian Girl or boy as for George, see
pages 46 and 48
primrose cutter
stamens
leaf cutters
blossom plunger cutter
heart cutter

1 First draw the initial. Make sure that your dough is particularly well kneaded when you are making this type of initial, especially when shaping a letter with curves, such as B, D or P, as these tend to crack or dent if your dough is either too wet or too dry.

2 With perfectly kneaded dough and your little preparatory sketch to hand, roll out some ropes of dough in suitable lengths for your chosen initial, see page 11. The ropes should be about as wide as two fingers held together.

3 Initials made from ropes of dough always look more professional if the corners are mitred and joins at other angles are cut to fit. However, do not let this prospect frighten

Clown Initial and Initial with Figure, see page 90

Initial with Figure

Building up the figure around the initial: adding the petticoat over the bloomers.

Fixing the head above the arms.

you, because, unlike badly mitred wooden corners, mitres in dough can be gently coaxed into perfection using a modelling tool and with a bit of squeezing. Arrange the ropes of dough into the shape of your letter, making sure that all joins are dampened before fixing them together.

4   Following the instructions for either Victorian Girl, see page 46, or George, see page 48, build up the chosen figure on the initial. Decorate with the flowers of your choice. I have used a primrose cutter, added some fluffy stamens at the modelling stage, then painted the flower when baked to represent a dog-rose. I have also added leaves, forget-me-knots and the ubiquitous butterfly, see page 14.

5   When you have completed the arrangement, bake the initial at 145°C (290°F/Gas 1½) for 2½ hours.

Painting and Finishing

● Paint the face, hands, little doll, petticoat and stockings as for Victorian Girl, see page 48.

Paint the dress with a mixture of Red Ochre and white and decorate it with sprigs of flowers and leaves painted in a mixture of Cadmium Red, Ultramarine and white for the flowers, and Cadmium Yellow, Ultramarine and white for the leaves. The hair ribbon is painted using the same mixture as for the flowers.

Paint the leaves on the initial as for those on the dress. The forget-me-knots are painted in pinks and pale blues, made from Red Ochre and white, and Ultramarine and white. Paint the larger flowers white and, while still damp, edge them with a little pink made from Red Ochre and white. Blend in pink with a clean damp brush. Paint the stamens and the centres of the forget-me-knots with a touch of Cadmium Yellow.

Paint the butterfly in any exotic mixture of colours with some white or black spots on the wings, and antennae on the dough in front of the head.

The body and the little girl's shoes are best painted in Raw Umber. Varnish back and front several times.

BALLET DANCER ·INITIAL·

Take more than the usual amount of care when making the dough for a rounded initial. It needs to be firm and extremely well kneaded if you are to avoid the dents and cracks that bending such a large amount of dough can cause. However, the nature of salt dough is to look a little rugged and rustic, so there is no need to worry unduly if your models are not always absolutely faultless.

This ballet dancer filled the wide open space of the 'G' quite well, but the continuous curve of the letter looked a little barren until I added the ballet shoes.

> ¾ quantity Basic Dough, see page 10
> 15cm (6in) saucer
> cocktail stick (toothpick)
> garlic press
> small blossom plunger cutter
> 5cm (2in) round fluted cutter
> 2.5cm (1in) round cutter
> 1 length medium floristry wire
> small leaf cutter
> modelling tool
> 2 Hanging Hooks, see page 17

1   Place the saucer on a baking tray and draw around it with a pencil. Take a little more than half the dough and roll a rope that is about the width of two fingers and about 42.5cm (17in) long. Carefully transfer the rope of dough to

the baking tray and curve it around the pencil circle, leaving a gap of about 5cm (2in). Trim the lower end of the open circle, cutting it straight across with a sharp knife.

2   Roll a 5cm (2in) rope of similar thickness and fit it across the trimmed end of the letter with a little water.

3   Roll two thin, 5cm (2in) long ropes for the legs. Make these slightly tapered at one end and trim them diagonally at the other. Attach the tapered ends to the inside of the letter and the slanting ends together for the tops of the legs. Arrange the legs so that the doll will appear to be pirouetting when she is complete.

4   For the body, model a piece of dough about the size and shape of a walnut and fix it, point down, to the top of the legs. Roll out two ropes for the arms. Make these a little shorter and slightly thinner than the legs and model a hand at one end of each, see page 13. Cut the other ends at a slant and fix them in

place on the body, placing one hand on the crossbar of the letter and setting the other one out to one side.

5   Cut six 2.5cm (1in) lengths of floristry wire and carefully wrap the free hand around them, fixing them in place with a little water. Roll a small ball of dough for the head. Fix this to the body with a little water and mark two eyes and a mouth with a cocktail stick (toothpick). Attach a tiny ball of dough for the nose. Push some dough through a clay gun or garlic press to make the hair, see page 12, and attach it to the head.

6   Roll out most of the remaining dough to about 3mm ($\frac{1}{8}$in) thick. Cut out 12 small blossoms to decorate the hair and to make up the posy. Fix these in place with a little water on the wires in the hand and on her head.

7   Using the fluted cutter, cut out three circles of dough and remove the centre of each with the small round cutter. Frill the edges of the rings with a cocktail stick (tooth-

The tennis player initial is for an older gentleman who still fancies himself as a tennis player. It is a caricature of someone I know and I am sure that you will have great fun designing similar figures to give to friends.

INITIAL IDEAS

Decorated initials can be made and given to celebrate most personal moments of glory, from birthdays to barmitzvas, the passing of exams to retirements. They are extremely popular and seem to be equally acceptable whether the recipient is young or old, male or female.

Initials are particularly welcome as christening gifts, especially if a little dough scroll or circle is added so that the baby's name and birthday can be printed on it at the painting stage.

pick), see page 14, then cut and open out one of them so that you have a frilled strip rather than a circle. Attach the curved side of the strip across the body and up at the sides to the arms. Cut a 4cm (1½in) wedge from the second ring. Lay this over the first strip, placing it about 3mm (¼in) higher. Cut a 2.5cm (1in) wedge from the third strip and attach this over the first two in the same way. Lift the frills away from each other slightly to make the skirt look like a tutu and support any rebelliously floppy dough with small pieces of folded cooking foil. Roll a very thin rope of dough and drape this across the chest and around the neck of the figure.

8 Cut out and vein three leaves, see page 16, and place them symmetrically near the cross-bar to cover the join in the dough. Make three roses and two rosebuds, see page 15, and place these in the middle of the leaves.

9 To make the ballet shoes, roll two small ovals of dough and hollow them out slightly with a modelling tool. Attach the ballet shoes to the side of the initial, then decorate them with two tiny bows and four long strips of dough to represent ribbons.

10 Finally, attach two hanging hooks at the top and one at the bottom of the initial. Bake at 145°C (290°F/Gas 1½) for about 2½ hours.

Painting and Finishing

● Mix some flesh colour and paint the face and arms, see page 42. Add a little pale blue for the eyes and some red for the mouth.

Brush clean water onto the legs and dress to make them *slightly* damp. Mix a very little Lemon Yellow into watery Permanent White and paint the legs, the two under skirts and the top of the bodice. Add a very little Cadmium Red to the pale yellow and blend this into the colour on the bodice. Complete the bottom of the bodice in this colour and continue it over

the waist and about a third of the way down the top layer of the dress. Add a little Cadmium Red to the mixture and blend this into the last colour and a little further down the skirt. Add a little more red and blend this in a similar way to complete the skirt.

Paint one or two blossoms, a rose, rosebud and shoes with the colour used on the skirt.

Mix some of the other colours used for the dress and paint the posy, garland and roses.

Paint the whole letter with a mixture of white and Ultramarine, making sure that you mix enough paint to complete the whole thing before you start painting.

When the initial has dried paint the leaves Olive Green and add a little Lemon Yellow to this to paint the centres of all the blossoms. Finally, paint the ballet shoes Cadmium Red, adding a little white to complete the linings.

TENNIS PLAYER
·INITIAL·

¾ quantity Basic Dough, see page 10
plastic ruler
cocktail sticks (toothpicks)
garlic press • tweezers
3cm (1¼in) and 2cm (¾in) round cutters
2 lengths fine floristry wire
wire cutters
retracted ballpoint pen
small daisy cutter
modelling tool
butterfly cutter
2 Hanging Hooks, see page 17

1 Using half the dough, roll two ropes each about the width of two fingers. Roll one to about 14cm (5½in) long and the other to 9cm (3½in) *without trimming* the dough. This will give the ropes naturally rounded ends, which look more attractive than cut ends. If you have to trim the dough, hold your knife at an angle so that the surface of the rope is slightly proud of its base. Trim a small amount of dough from one end of the longest rope to make a straight edge and attach this to the middle of the shorter rope with a little water to form a 'T'.

2   Roll two fairly thin ropes 7.5cm (3in) long for the legs from a little of the remaining dough. Make sure that at least one end of each rope is rounded. Then form an indentation in each rope, 2cm ($\frac{3}{4}$in) away from the rounded end, by gently rolling your finger across the dough. Dab a little water in these indentations with a brush, then push the rounded end up so that it stands at right angles to the rest of the leg and forms a foot.

3   Roll out half of the remaining dough to about 3mm ($\frac{1}{8}$in) thick. Using a sharp knife and a well-floured ruler, cut two 6.5cm $\times$ 3.5cm ($2\frac{1}{2} \times 1\frac{1}{2}$in) rectangles. Fit one of these around the top of each leg to represent shorts and secure them at the back with a little water.

4   To make socks, cut another two 5 $\times$ 3.5cm (2 $\times$ 1$\frac{1}{2}$in) rectangles. Using a cocktail stick (toothpick) roll and pleat the dough so that the pleats are parallel with the longest edges of the rectangles. Leave the top 6mm ($\frac{1}{4}$in) of each piece flat and fold it back before making vertical indentations to represent ribbing. Wrap these around the bottoms of the legs, pushing them well down on the shoes, before securing them at the back with water.

5   Make two very small balls of dough and flatten them slightly before attaching them to the legs, just below the shorts to represent knees. Use a damp brush to smooth the edges of the balls of dough into the legs. Trim the top ends of the legs and shorts diagonally, so that the highest point of the diagonal is on the outside of each.

6   Model a rounded shape for the body. If you want a tall and slim figure, make an oval

shape. Pinch the body in slightly at both ends, where the arms and legs are going to fit, then attach the legs with a little water. Dampen the side of the figure slightly and press him against the letter.

7   Roll out two thin ropes of dough for the arms, making sure that they are in proportion to the rest of the body, and make hands at one end, see page 13. Cut a strip of rolled-out dough about 2cm ($\frac{3}{4}$in) deep and 7.5cm (3in) long. Attach this around the top of the left arm to make a sleeve. Trim the top of the sleeve and arm at a slant and attach it to the top of the body so that the arm is raised.

8   Curve a thin strip of dough around the top of the body to represent the neck of the T-shirt. Indicate the ribbing by indenting this with the back of a knife. Make the ribbing at the bottom of the shirt in a similar way.

9   Cut the hand from the second arm and attach it to the other side of the initial, leaving some of the fingers free to hold the string bag. Make the head from a round, smooth piece of dough and mark the eyes and mouth with a cocktail stick (toothpick). Attach a very small ball of dough for the nose. Fit the head in place on top of the body and add a few wisps of garlic-press hair, see page 12.

10   Cut one large and one small circle of rolled-out dough. Press the larger circle out a little between your finger and thumb, then turn in a small hem all around the edge. Cut the smaller circle in half and attach one half to the hemmed side of the larger circle so that it protrudes from underneath like the peak of a cap. Turn the dough over and place it on the model's head.

11   Make seven smooth balls of dough, a suitable size for tennis balls, and pile them up against the far side of the initial, a little way below the hand. Press some dough through

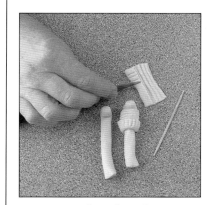

Making the socks.

95

DIFFICULT LETTERS

The letter 'T', like 'L' and 'J', is very suitable for standing figures but it is not so easy to fit in the figure if you are dealing with curved letters, like 'G' and 'Q', or letters with bars, like 'A' and 'H'.

Rounded letters work best with the figure leaning back and curving into the letter, while barred letters look good with the model draped nonchalantly over the crossbar. So you can still decorate initials for the likes of Quentin and Hubert if you take time to make a small preparatory sketch to find the best position for the figure before modelling the dough.

Rogue letters like 'K', 'M' and 'N' take a little more thought than simple letter shapes, but it is always possible to fit the figure in somewhere. Remember that while you do not have to show all the body, you must take care not to obscure the shape of the letter.

the garlic press. Then use well-floured tweezers to lay single strands of dough across the balls to form a string bag. Take some of the vertical strands up beyond the balls and tuck them under the unattached fingers of the hand to form a handle. Secure all the pieces with a little water as you work.

12 To make the tennis racket, roll out a thin rope of dough and form it into an oval to make the racket head. Cut several short lengths of wire and use these to represent the strings of the racket, embedding the ends in the dough frame. Roll a thin rope of dough to represent the handle and attach the head of the racket to it. Place the other end of the handle into the upraised hand of the model. Bring the head of the racket around so that it rests on the top of the initial and attach it with a little water. Roll out another thin rope of dough and lay it on top of the frame as decoration, marking it with a retracted ballpoint pen.

13 Cut out three daisies and press their petals out a little with a modelling tool before attaching them to the initial over the join between the upright and crossbar. Press a small ball of dough into each daisy centre and prick these all over with a cocktail stick (toothpick).

14 Cut out the butterfly, flute its wings and make a body, see page 14. Arrange the butterfly on the initial. Attach one hanging hook in the top and another at the bottom of the initial. Bake at 145°C (290°F/Gas 1½) for about 2½ hours.

Painting and Finishing

● Mix up a little flesh colour and paint the face, arms and legs, see page 42. Redden the knees a little and make the face look more hot and bothered than normal if you like.

When dry, paint the hair, moustache and eyebrows with a little thin Raw Umber. Paint the eyes with a mixture of Ultramarine and white and the mouth with a wash of Cadmium Red. Take a clean brushful of water and slightly dampen all the items of dress to be painted white, then wash on a thin, but opaque, layer of white. Allow the white to dry before painting the trim on the sweater and socks with one stripe of Olive Green and one of Spectrum Violet. It is easier to keep these lines straight using a rigger brush, see page 112.

Use a mixture of Lemon Yellow and a touch of Olive Green for the tennis balls – do not worry too much if you smudge this colour on the string bag, the Spectrum Violet will easily cover it up. When the balls are quite dry, use a fine brush and paint the string bag carefully with Spectrum Violet.

Paint the daises white and while they are wet smudge a little diluted Cadmium Red mixed with white onto the tips of the petals. Paint the centres of the daisies Lemon Yellow, smudged with a touch of diluted Cadmium Red around one side. Mix a small amount of Lemon Yellow into the Olive Green and paint groups of leaves around the daisies.

The butterfly is painted with a mixture of Cadmium Red and Cadmium Yellow, with a touch of pure yellow dabbed onto it while it is still wet. Tinge the edge with some pale blue when the first colour is dry and paint the body with Raw Umber, with lines and spots of black and white. Add two white spots, encircled with black on the wings and paint two antennae on the dough just in front of the head.

Paint the tennis racket with Burnt Sienna. Use a mixture of Ultramarine and white to paint the handle and to decorate the racket. The studs around the head of the racket are painted in silver but you could just as easily use white.

CHRISTMAS DECORATIONS

Christmas decorations are always fun to make and many of the ideas in this section are quite simple and ideal for beginners. You can begin by making cherubs, Christmas stockings or teddy bear tree decorations, and then progress onto a charming Nativity scene, a model to be treasured for years to come.

· CHRISTMAS LABELS ·

$\frac{1}{4}$ quantity Basic Dough, see page 10
plastic ruler
thick plastic drinking straw
small holly leaf cutter
small bird cutter
small leaf cutter
small primrose cutter
modelling tool
stamens • cocktail stick (toothpick)
about 30cm (12in) narrow ribbon or
decorative string

1 Roll out half the dough to 6mm ($\frac{1}{4}$in) thick. Flour a plastic ruler well and use it as a guide for cutting out two 6.5 × 4cm (2$\frac{1}{2}$ × 1$\frac{1}{2}$in) rectangles of dough with a sharp knife. Trim one end of both rectangles to a point to make a label shape and then, using a plastic straw, make holes for the ribbon in the pointed ends.

2 Roll out some thinner dough and cut out two holly leaves. Indent a central vein in both of these with the back of a knife and fix them end to end on one of the labels, leaving enough room for the robin to sit on top of them. Make three small balls of dough to represent holly berries and place these in the middle of the leaves.

3 Use a small bird cutter to cut out the robin and sit him on top of the berries. Make a wing with the small leaf cutter and notch one side slightly to represent feathers. Mark the robin's eye with a cocktail stick (toothpick).

4 For the second label, cut out and mark veins on five more holly leaves, then arrange them in a ring, with their ends pointing inwards. Make five small balls of dough for holly berries and pile these up in the middle of the leaves.

5 Cut out a Christmas rose using a small primrose cutter and press out the petals with the rounded end of a modelling tool, see page 16. Fix the Christmas rose close to the holly and push four small stamens into the middle.

6 Bake the labels at 145°C (290°F/Gas 1$\frac{1}{2}$) for about 1 hour. Look at them repeatedly during baking and if they show any signs of

Christmas Puddings
Simple balls of Basic Dough, see page 10, are placed on circles of dough to make these tree decorations. Fix a hanging hook in the top of them.

CRAFT TIP

Varnish and dry the back of the dough, then stick on self-adhesive labels on which to write messages.

Christmas Labels

97

Father Christmas

Building up Father Christmas and showing the technique used to create the fur texture.

bubbling either prick them with a needle or lay something heavy, like the metal handle of a knife, on them.

Painting and Finishing

● Paint all the holly leaves with Olive green and all the berries with Spectrum Red. Continue using the red to paint the robin's chest and a line all around the top of both labels. Encircle the hole with another line of red and decorate the sides of the label with dots in the same colour.

Paint the rest of the robin with Raw Umber, adding a yellow eye and beak.

Use pure Permanent White to paint the Christmas rose and, while this is still wet, wash a watery mixture of Olive Green and Lemon Yellow into the middle of the flower.

Finish the labels by brushing a little gold onto the ends of the leaves and by painting a gold line just inside the red one.

Varnish and when this is dry thread coloured ribbon or string through the holes.

·FATHER CHRISTMAS·

¾ quantity Basic Dough, see page 10
modelling tool
garlic press
cocktail stick (toothpick)
Hanging Hook, see page 17

1 Roll two 9cm (3½in) long, finger-thick ropes of dough, see page 11. Roll your finger 2.5cm (1in) from the end of one of them to make a groove. Dampen the groove and push the end up to form a foot. Repeat with the other rope. Trim the other ends on the slant and fix the diagonal cuts together on a baking sheet.

2 Roll out some dough thinly and cut a rectangle measuring 16.5 × 4cm (6½ ×

1½in). Make a thin, 16.5cm (6½in) long rope and fix it along one long edge of the rectangle. Make two pleats, facing each other, and close to the middle on the opposite side. Fix the pleats with a little water, then dust them with flour and roll their top edge to make them less bulky. Lay this 'skirt' across the top 2.5cm (1in) of the legs, tucking under each side neatly.

3 For the body, mould a small handful of dough into a smooth egg shape. Wet the back of the dough and arrange it so that 2.5cm (1in) of the lower edge of the 'skirt' protrudes.

4 Cut two 6.5cm × 12mm (2½×½in) strips of rolled-out dough and trim the end of one to a point. Overlap the pointed end on the edge of the second strip by 12mm (½in) to make a belt. Fix the belt in position to cover the join between the body and the skirt. Cut a 12mm (½in) square of dough, then cut a smaller square from the middle of this to form a buckle. Place this on the pointed side of the belt, adding a tiny rope of dough to represent the fastener. Use a modelling tool to make several eyelets in the belt.

5 Roll two 9cm (3½in) long ropes of dough and model hands at one end, see page 13. Trim the other ends diagonally and fix to the shoulders. Make two thin, 5cm (2in) long ropes of dough and arrange around the bottom of the arms as cuffs, then place the hands on the belt.

6 Mould the head in proportion to the body and attach it to the shoulders. Use a small ball of dough for the nose and indent the eyes and mouth with the modelling tool. Flatten two small balls of dough for cheeks and arrange them on the face, then soften their edges with the modelling tool. Push some dough through a garlic press to make a beard and some hair.

7 Make a hat as for the Christmas Teddy, see page 100. Arrange two 7.5cm (3in) ropes of

Father Christmas, Christmas Teddy, see page 100, and a holly wreath, see page 101

dough on the legs to represent the tops of boots and place two small balls of dough on the coat for buttons. Roughen all the rope trimmings using a cocktail stick (toothpick) to simulate fur. Push a hanging hook into the hat and bake at 145°C (290°F/Gas 1½) for 2 hours.

Painting and Finishing

● Make some flesh colour for the face and hands and paint as for the Victorian Doll, see page 48. Using pure Spectrum Red, paint the trousers, coat and hat but not the fur trimmings. Paint the boots with Lamp Black and the belt with Raw Umber.

Allow to dry thoroughly, then paint all the fur white and the beard, belt-buckle and eyebrows silver.

·CHRISTMAS TEDDIES·

The quantity of dough below is sufficient to make four teddies.
¾ quantity Basic Dough, see page 10
teddy bear cutter
cocktail stick (toothpick)
4 Hanging Hooks, see page 17

1   Roll out two-thirds of the dough to 6mm (½in) thick. Cut out four teddies and place them on a baking sheet.
2   Roll out the remaining dough a little thinner and cut out four triangles with 7.5cm (3in) sides to make hats. Wrap one side of a triangle of dough around one head, over one ear. Fold the other two sides under to form a point at the top of the hat and bend this over. Repeat with the remaining hats.
3   Roll eight thin 6.5cm (2½in) long ropes of dough, see page 11, and wrap these around the bears' legs to represent the fur at the top of their boots. Roll four similar ropes, 7.5cm

(3in) long and use these to trim the edges of the hats, then add small balls of dough for bobbles. Roughen the bobble and the ropes of dough using a cocktail stick (toothpick) to simulate fur. Attach hanging hooks and bake at 145°C (290°F/Gas 1½) for 1 hour.

Painting and Finishing

● Paint features and boots with Lamp Black and the hats in Spectrum Red. When dry, paint the fur trimmings Permanent White.

Christmas Tree
A Christmas tree cutter was used to stamp out the hanging decoration in Basic Dough, see page 10. Once the parcels, decorations and a hanging hook were fixed in place the tree was baked for about 1 hour. When painted and varnished, gold cord was used to complete the decoration.

*Making a small wreath for the
Christmas tree. This is modelled from
a simple twist of dough, see
page 12, made to 20cm (8in) in
length. Arrange holly leaves and
berries over the join in the dough and
fit a hanging hook behind the leaves.
Paint with glaze, avoiding the leaves
and berries, then sprinkle with poppy
seeds. Bake at 145°C (290°/
Gas 1½) for 1½ hours.
Paint the leaves and berries, varnish
and add a bow.*

·WINGED HEAD CHERUB·

*1 quantity Basic Dough, see page 10
leaf cutters
modelling tool • garlic press
Hanging Hook, see page 17*

1   Make a 17.5cm (7in) rope from a quarter of the dough, see page 11. Taper the ends and flatten the rope with a rolling pin, then tilt the tapered ends up slightly on a baking sheet.

2   Roll out the remaining dough and cut out several leaves in all sizes. Mark veins on the leaves using the back of a knife and arrange them on the rope, overlapping each other with the smallest leaves at the tapered ends and the largest ones towards the middle. Leave a space about 4cm (1½in) across in the centre and towards the base of the rope.

3   Mould a large, slightly flattened ball of dough for the head and place it in the space on the rope. Tuck two large leaves under the head on either side of the chin. Lay two medium leaves on top, then add two very small leaves on top of those.

4   Mould a small ball of dough for the nose and place it in the middle of the face. Mark the mouth with the end of the modelling tool. Arrange two small, flattened balls of dough on the face for cheeks. Smooth the cheek edges with the modelling tool and a damp brush.

5   Push several short lengths of dough through a garlic press to represent hair. Fix a hanging hook in the dough and bake at 145°C (290°F/Gas 1½) for about 2 hours.

Painting and Finishing

● Leave the dough natural adding a little watery Rose Madder to the cheeks, mouth and chin. Paint two Permanent White

CRAFT TIP

If you want a rosy cherub, like the one illustrated, give the dough a coating of Egg Glaze, see page 11, before baking and tint the cheeks, knees and feet with some watery pink paint while the glaze is still wet.

Garlanded Cherub
Position of wings and legs for the cherub.

Blending the knees into the legs.

lozenge shapes for eyes, remembering to paint the left one first if you are right handed and vice versa. While this is drying, paint the wings white. Make pale blue by mixing Ultramarine and white, and some pink by adding a little Rose Madder to white. Tip all the feathers with a little of each while the white is still damp. Use the pale blue to paint an iris in each eye. When the wings are quite dry edge the feathers with Gold and paint the hair with the same colour. Finish by putting a black dot in the centre of the iris and by outlining the eyes and the eyebrows.

·GARLANDED CHERUB·

½ quantity Basic Dough, see page 10
Wing Template, see page 138
thin card
modelling tool
small holly leaf cutter
blossom plunger cutter

1 For the legs, roll two finger-thick ropes each about 6.5cm (2½in) long, from a small handful of dough, see page 11. Trim one end of each rope diagonally and fix the two diagonal cuts side-by-side, shortest sides inwards on a baking sheet. Trim feet-ends on the slant, with the longest sides together in the middle. Make four small cuts into the trimmed edges to represent toes, then fix a small flattened ball of dough halfway up each leg to represent knees.

2 Trace the wing template, then cut it out in thin card. Roll out one-third of the remaining dough and press the template down on it to leave a clear impression when removed. Carefully cut around the imprint, then transfer the wings to the baking sheet, above the legs.

3 Dampen the wings and leg tops. Mould a piece of dough into the shape of a large smooth egg and press this down on the wings and the tops of the legs to represent the body. Mark a belly button using the modelling tool.

4 Roll two pencil-thin, 7.5cm (3in) long ropes of dough and flatten one end of each to make hands, see page 13. Trim the other end of the dough diagonally and fix to the shoulders. Dampen the inside of the hands and lay these on the body.

5 Mould a ball of dough for the head in proportion to the body and mark a smiling mouth using the modelling tool. Flatten a small ball of dough on either side of the mouth to represent cheeks and add a very small ball of dough for a nose. Mark the eyes with the modelling tool. Fix the head on the body and wings, then decorate with small coils of dough to represent hair.

6 Make the garland with small holly leaves and blossoms, adding a few very small balls of dough for holly berries. Fix a hanging hook on the side so that the cherub appears to be flying when he is hung up. Bake at 145°C (290°F/Gas 1½) for about 1 hour.

Painting and Finishing

● If you did not make your cherub rosy before baking, take some very watery Rose Madder and add a little wash to the cheeks, mouth, toes and knees.

Paint the holly leaves with thin Olive Green and the berries with Spectrum Red. Use Permanent White to paint the wings and add a little pale blue, made by mixing Ultramarine and white, to the edges while still wet. Edge the blue with a Rose Madder and white mix, then finish by just tipping the edges with a little Gold and adding a few decorative gold dots. Paint the hair Gold. Paint the little blossoms white, adding pale green in the centre.

Winged Head Cherub, see page 101, and Garlanded Cherub

Bending and attaching the trotting leg.

· ROCKING HORSE ·

The following quantity will make two rocking horses. Divide the dough in half before following the instructions.

½ quantity Basic Dough, see page 10
2.5cm (1in) round cutter
retracted ballpoint pen
modelling tool
Hanging Hook, see page 17
30cm (12in) narrow red ribbon

1 Model a handful of dough into a pear shape with a slightly elongated neck. Flatten this slightly and put it to one side. Make three pencil-thin, 5cm (2in) long ropes and trim one end of each at a slant. Use the back of a knife to indent a line around each rope, about 6mm (¼in) above the trimmed end, to make a hoof.

2 Lay two of the legs on a baking try, with the hooves about 9cm (2½in) apart and the rest of the legs slanting inwards. Wet the tops of the legs and lay the pear-shaped piece on top for the body, so that it overlaps them by about 12mm (½in). The body should be slightly tilted with the neck on your left.

3 Round the end of the third leg opposite the hoof, if necessary, by modelling it with your fingers. Shape the leg into a trotting position and fix it on top of the body so that it lays just ahead of the other front leg. Model the fourth leg in a similar way, but this time make it 6.5cm (2½in) long and allow it to become much wider above the first 3cm (1¼in). Make a hoof at the narrow end and mould the wide end into a round haunch. Secure it to the rear of the body. The leg should lay in front of the other back leg.

4 Roll a 15cm (6in) pencil-thin rope and flatten it with your fingers before curving it under the hooves of the horse, so that three of them touch it. Fix the three legs to the rocker with a little water. Decorate it around the edge with the retracted ballpoint pen.

5 Model a small piece of dough into an oval for the head. Indent across the top of the narrower end with the back of a knife to mark the mouth. Secure the head on the body. Use the pointed end of one of your modelling tools to mark two nostrils and a slight indentation at either end of the mouth.

6 Flatten two very small balls of dough and secure these on the face as eyes. Indent them horizontally across the middle, with the back of a knife. Use the 2.5cm (1in) round cutter to cut a circle of thinly rolled-out dough and divide it into four wedges. Round the points on two wedges slightly to make ears.

7 Roll a very thin rope of dough about 4cm (1½in) long and fix it across the horse's face as a nose band. Make an indented pattern on the nose band with the pointed end of a modelling tool and make a tiny ring of dough to go at one end of it. Use the 2.5cm (1in) cutter to cut out

a circle of rolled-out dough and cut it in half. Take one of the semi-circles and thin and enlarge it slightly between your fingers and thumb. Place this on the horse's back as a saddle and indent the edges of it with the retracted ballpoint pen. Cut a thin strip of dough about 4cm (1½in) long; secure it from the saddle under the horse's stomach.

8   Roll several long, thin and tapering ropes for the horse's tail and secure these in place in a bunch. Make similar, but shorter, ropes for the mane and attach them along the neck and between his ears. Finally, roll a very thin rope for reins and loop this through the ring on the nose band and over the horse's back. Put a hanging hook in the top of the saddle. Bake at 145°C (290°F/Gas 1½) for about 1 hour.

Painting and Finishing

● Make up watery grey by adding black to Permanent White and paint the horse. While this is still wet, mix pale pink from white and a touch of Flame Red, add it to the muzzle and blend it into the rest of his face. Add a little more black to the grey and paint uneven patches across the top of his back and legs.

Use pure white to paint the lower half of his eyes and dry. Use black to make a dot in the centre of the white and to run along the eyelid edge. Use black on the hooves and reins.

Paint the nose band, saddle and girth in Flame Red and the rocker in Fir Green. When dry, paint on Gold decoration. Use the gold to paint a wavy line down the middle of the rocker and to paint the nose band ring.

Varnish and dry. Loop half the ribbon through the hanging hook and knot the ends together. Let the knotted end hang down behind the horse and tie a bow around the base of the looped ribbon, close to the top of the hook.

CHRISTMAS · STOCKINGS ·

½ quantity Basic Dough, see page 10
round-ended modelling tool
plastic drinking straw
garlic press or clay gun
cocktail stick (toothpick)
30cm (12in) narrow red ribbon
15cm (6in) narrow gold card
fast-drying glue

1   Take a small handful of dough and make a fairly thick rope measuring about 15cm (6in) long. Mould one end into a stocking foot by squaring it off slightly with your fingers, then pulling one corner into more of a point for the toe, while bending it over a little to make an instep.

2   Insert the round-ended modelling tool into the top and push out the sides of the rope until you have widened the top of the stocking to about 10cm (4in) in circumference. Pinch the back of the stocking top and pull it up gently until it is about 2.5cm (1in) higher than the front. Make a hole in the back, quite near the top, with the plastic drinking straw.

3   Put your fingers into the stocking to support it, then make small indentations with the back of a knife around the edge to simulate ribbing. Still keeping your fingers in place, go around the stocking again, making small holes at the base of the ribbing with a cocktail stick (toothpick).

RAG DOLL STOCKING

4   To fill the rag doll stocking, place it on the baking try and mould a little rectangular dough parcel. Place this on end in the back of the stocking and make a ball of dough to go in front of it. Push them both down into the stocking a little so that they hold it open.

Walking Stick
The bright walking stick is made from red, green and white ropes of Bread Dough, see page 11, twisted together and curved into the shape of the handle.
Add a hanging hook at the top. When dry, the dough is given an additional coat of paint before being varnished. Gold cord and a double bow of red ribbon decorate the walking stick which is ready to hang on the Christmas tree.

5 Make a small oval of dough for the doll's torso and place this in the stocking so that it slightly overlaps the edge, but is down far enough not to need any skirt or legs. Make two very thin 2.5cm (1in) long ropes for the doll's arms and slightly flatten the rounded ends of them to make simple hands. Secure these on the body so that they flop out of the stocking. Then make a small ball of dough for the head. Secure the head at a floppy angle and mark two eyes and a mouth with a cocktail stick (toothpick). Make the nose from a tiny ball of dough and the hair from dough that has been pressed through the garlic press or – better still – extruded through a clay gun. Hair made with a clay gun is finer.

TEDDY BEAR STOCKING

6 First put a small square parcel of dough into the stocking, then add a small ball of dough to represent an orange. Prick the orange lightly all over with a cocktail stick (toothpick).

Make a small oval of dough for the teddy's body and indent a line down the middle with the back of a knife. Put this into the stocking so that it is leaning out.

7 Make a head from a small pear-shaped piece of dough. Fix a tiny ball of dough at the pointed end of the pear shape to represent the teddy's nose, then fix the head on the body. Mark two eyes with a cocktail stick (toothpick) and make two ears by pressing the rounded end of the modelling tool into two small balls of dough. Secure the ears on the head. Then make two thin ropes of dough, about 2cm ($\frac{3}{4}$in) long, for the arms. Attach these so that one is flopping over the side. Model a tennis racket out of a small circle of dough and a thin rope. Stick this, head up, into the back of the stocking.

8 Bake the stockings together at 145°C (290°F/Gas 1$\frac{1}{2}$) for about 1 hour.

Painting and Finishing

RAG DOLL STOCKING

● Paint the stocking white, apart from the toe, heel and ribbing; dry. Starting with the ribbing and using Flame Red, paint three stripes fairly close together around the stocking; paint more red stripes further apart on leg and foot. Paint the heel and toe solid red. Paint alternate stripes in Fir Green. The ribbed section is red and green, the rest is red, white and green.

Mix up flesh colour, see page 42, and paint the doll's face and about three quarters of her arms. Paint her body and short sleeves in pure Cadmium Yellow. When dry, paint white spots and cuffs on her dress.

Divide the ball up into eight sections. Using Saffron Green, Ultramarine, orange made from Cadmium Red and Cadmium Yellow, and pale blue made from Ultramarine and white, paint pairs of opposite sections in the same colour. Paint a dot of Flame Red where all the sections meet. Finally, paint the oblong box in pure Rose Pink.

TEDDY BEAR STOCKING

● Paint the stocking Flame Red and dry. Paint a stripe around the ribbing, the toe and heel in pure white. Paint the square box Saffron Green and the orange by mixing Cadmium Red and Yellow. Use Yellow Ochre to paint the teddy and the middle of the tennis racket; dry. Paint Jet Black strings. Paint a small black cross in the middle of the orange. Paint the bear's nose, eyes and claws black. Paint the handle and frame of the racket in Fir Green. Varnish and dry. Thread half the ribbon through each hole and tie the ends in a bow in front of the hole. Add a dab of glue to secure the bow.

Glue gold cord and bows on the boxes.

· GINGERBREAD ·
MEN AND WOMEN

These rather sophisticated figures are made with biscuit (cookie) cutters; however, with just a few additions, they make quite witty Christmas tree gifts or place-name markers, especially if you can make them look *something* like your guests.

> ½ quantity Basic Dough, see page 10
> gingerbread man and woman cutters
> garlic press
> fine sieve
> cocktail stick (toothpick)
> 4 Hanging Hooks, see page 17

1 Roll out dough to 6mm (¼ in) thick and cut out two gingerbread men and two gingerbread women. Lay them on a baking tray, arranging their arms and legs in different positions to give them some individuality and expression.
2 To make hair for the lady in blue, push some dough through a sieve, see page 13, and arrange it on her head in a short style. Make a neat 'bobbed' style for the lady in green, from dough that has been passed through the garlic press; use the same method to make shorter styles for the men.
3 Form two small balls of dough into noses for the ladies and model two small wedges of dough to make slightly more curved or aquiline noses for the men.
4 Give one of the men a droopy moustache and mark a mouth beneath it by making a hole with the cocktail stick (toothpick). Give the other man a fuller mouth by attaching a tiny rope of dough and indenting it along the middle. Give the same man protruding eyes and drooping eyelids, by placing two tiny balls of dough in the correct positions and indenting them across the middle.
5 Give each of the ladies a bust by placing two small balls of dough side by side on their chests. Place a hanging hook in each head and bake the gingerbread people at 145°C (290°F/Gas 1½) for about 1 hour.

Painting and Finishing

● Add a very small amount of Ultramarine to white to make a very pale blue and then use it to paint two almond shapes to represent the whites of the eyes on each of the ladies. Do the same to the man with the moustache, but make the outside edges of his eyes droop down a little. Paint only the lower half of the bulging eyes on the other man.

Add a little more blue to the mixture and paint blue circles in each of the eyes to represent the irises, then allow this to dry before encircling it with a thin line of black.

Paint a small black dot in the middle of each iris and then draw around the almond shapes on the two ladies in the same colour. Add a few eyelashes to their eyes and paint eyebrows and a beauty spot the same colour.

Paint a far thinner line around the almond

shape of the eyes on the man with the moustache and give him some thin, and slightly quizzical, eyebrows. Paint a black line through the indentation across the eyes of the second man to represent eyelashes and give him some slightly raised eyebrows.

Mix up some very watery Cadmium Red and blush some onto the cheeks of all the characters; brush this red across the bridge of the nose on the man with the moustache and on the mouth of the other man. Allow this to dry and then paint the mouths of the ladies with pure Cadmium Red.

To finish painting the lady in green, mix up some very watery black paint and wash this over her legs. Allow it to dry and then criss-cross her legs with fine black lines to represent fish-net stockings. Paint simple black shoe shapes at the end of her legs. Finally, mix up some pure Viridian and paint a dress with long sleeves and a low, square neck line.

Paint the lady in blue's legs with some very watery Ultramarine. Mix some more Ultramarine and white together to obtain a mid-blue for her off-the-shoulder dress. Add two fine shoulder straps to the dress. When the legs are quite dry paint her shoes in Red Ochre.

Take some pure Red Ochre and paint a long, open, dinner-jacket shape on the man with the moustache. Allow this to dry before painting black lapels, cuffs, pocket flaps and buttonholes. Mix a little white into the black to make grey, and paint the same man's trousers. When these are dry, paint his shoes black and his shirt white.

Paint an Ultramarine, cardigan-shaped jacket on the second man and paint some pure Viridian trousers. When both colours are completely dry, take some more Viridian and some Red Ochre and paint a tartan design on the jacket, see page 112. Mix some black and white to make grey for his shoes and leave it to dry. Paint toe caps and laces on the shoes in a slightly paler grey.

Give all the figures a coat of clear poly-urethane gloss varnish and allow them to dry.

You need such small amounts of trimmings to decorate these little figures that it makes more sense to use whatever you have, rather than buying large quantities of all the items I have used in an effort to make exact copies of these dolls. You will probably find that you already have all sorts of suitable sequins, braids and beads. Nevertheless I include the details of materials below to give you some idea of what you can utilize.

Lady in Green   The frill on her dress and turban are made from very fine Japanese paper serviettes, glued on with P.V.A glue. She has a small piece of Ostrich feather held in place on her hat with a large sequin, and a matching sequin on her dress. A row of very small pearls are attached around her neck.

Lady in Blue   The blue lady also has a frill on her dress made from a Japanese paper serviette, this time it is bound with some gold gift-wrapping ribbon. The same type of ribbon is glued around the top of her dress and she has two gold shell-shaped sequins for earrings.

Man with The Moustache   I have trimmed two small pieces from a paper doily to make the frills for his dress shirt and added three black beads for the buttons. His tie and cummerband are made from fine Japanese paper serviettes and his three coat buttons are black sequins.

Man in The Tartan Jacket   I cut a piece of white floristry ribbon into a triangular shape and folded the top over to make a polo-necked shirt, then glued it on with P.V.A. glue. A small piece of the same ribbon makes his handkerchief, and his buttons are three gold sequins.

CHRISTMAS ·TREE ANGEL·

about $\frac{1}{3}$ quantity Bread Dough, see page 10
waxed paper
cocktail sticks (toothpicks)
P.V.A. glue
modelling tool
Hanging Hook, see page 17
piece of polystyrene
retracted ballpoint pen
garlic press

1 Take a small piece of the dough and roll two thin ropes each about 5cm (2in) long. Flatten one end of both of them slightly and make a pair of feet, see page 13. Make some thin arms and hands, about 4cm (1½in) long, see page 13, and put these and the legs to dry on a piece of waxed paper.

2 Roll a small ball of dough for the head. Mark the eyes and a small hole for the mouth with a cocktail stick (toothpick). Make a tiny ball of dough for the nose and glue this in place. Place the head on a cocktail stick and stand it in a piece of polystyrene until it dries.

3 To make the trumpet, roll a tapering rope about 2.5 cm (1in) long. Open up the broad end by inserting a modelling tool and then roll this until the dough is hollowed and widened into a trumpet shape. Put this to one side to dry.

4 Roll out another small piece of dough thinly between two sheets of waxed paper. Cut out two triangles with equal sides of 3cm (1¼in) each. Cut three fairly deep notches in one side of each triangle to make wings, and then indent a pattern on these feathery pieces with the retracted pen.

5 When the legs are dry, take a small ball of dough and flatten it out into a circle large enough to make the angel's gown. Indent the edge of the circle with the ballpoint pen and then curve and glue it into a cone. Glue

the legs inside the gown so that the front of the feet show beneath the edge of the dough on the side without the join. Push a short hanging hook into the back of the gown.

6 Use smaller circles of dough to make sleeves in a similar way to the gown. Then lay all these pieces to dry on waxed paper.

7 When the head is dry, flatten two very small balls and glue them onto the face as puffed-out cheeks. Thin the edges of the cheeks and mould them onto the face.

8 Keep the head fixed into the polystyrene on the end of the cocktail stick (toothpick), while you gradually glue on strands of dough from a garlic press to build up hair.

9 Glue the thin end of the trumpet into the mouth of the angel and support the other end on crumpled paper until the glue has dried.

Christmas Tree Angel

CRAFT TIP

Unlike salt dough figures, bread dough people have to be made up of separate pieces which are assembled only when dry. This means that they take a lot longer to make and that care has to be taken over the proportions of all the parts.

Gluing the legs into the gown.

Moulding the cheeks onto the face.

10 When dry, glue the head onto the point of the cone-shaped gown and attach the tops of the arms on each side of it, so that they are stretched out in the same direction as the trumpet. Glue the hands to the trumpet. Attach the wings to the angel's back and dry.

Painting and Finishing

● Mix up flesh colour, see page 42 and paint the angel's arms, legs and face. Add a little more Cadmium Red to the mixture and blend this into the cheeks, fingertips and toes.

Paint the gown and wings white. Add a little Ultramarine to make pale blue. Blend this into the ends of the wings while they are damp. Make pink by mixing white and Alizarin Crimson, then blend this into the pale blue wing tips. Use pale blue to paint the angel's eyes. Paint the decoration on the gown and wings, trumpet and hair with gold.

Varnish with spirit-based acrylic varnish or oil-based clear gloss polyurethane varnish.

· NATIVITY SCENE ·

It is worth taking trouble with this project which could well become a family heirloom. Although it will spend most of its time packed away in a box along with other Christmas decorations, once a year its moment will come – and who knows how many generations will admire your artistry or even try to emulate it when the paint begins to fade?

$1\frac{1}{4}$ quantities Basic Dough, see page 10
plastic ruler
clay gun or garlic press
retracted ballpoint pen
5cm (2in) round fluted cutter
modelling tool • kitchen foil
fine sieve • medium daisy cutter
2 Hanging Hooks, see page 17
Egg Glaze, see page 11
rigger brush

1 Take a handful of dough and make a 20cm (8in) long, finger-thick rope, see page 11. Lay this on a baking try. Make two more ropes about twice as thick and 15cm (6in) long. Score these lengthways with the side of a ruler to represent columns, then stand one at each end of the first rope and secure with a little water. Make a rope similar to the first and lay it across the top of the columns. To shape the roof, roll one more finger-thick rope, about 25cm (10in) long, and fix its ends to the ends of the rope across the top of the columns. Curve the rope upwards so that it forms a domed roof.

2 Pass dough through a clay gun or garlic press to make short lengths of thatching for the roof. Gradually build up a thatch to cover the domed rope and fill the roof space, also cover the rope across the bottom of the roof.

3 To make the back of Mary's chair, if you are using a clay gun, fit the disc that resembles

Nativity Scene

STRIPES AND CHECKS

Use a rigger brush to make these designs. If you have never used a rigger before, I would practise first on a piece of paper. Make the paint quite runny, but still opaque, and completely cover the long hairs in your brush with it. Wipe the brush on the side of your palette to make sure that all the hairs are lying straight and then draw your lines, using as much of the length of the brush as you can.

a clover leaf and twist the dough as it comes through. Cut two 5cm (2in) lengths of the twist and lay them about 2.5cm (1in) apart in the middle of the stable. Place a tiny ball of dough on each. If you are not using a clay gun, make two small ropes with a ball on each.

4   Model a small figure with a long skirt but no petticoat, see Carol Singers. Make the head but do not mark the eyes and mouth, just model a small nose. Make a very thin rope of dough for the neckline of the dress and indent it with a retractable ballpoint pen. Use the same method to decorate the hem of the dress.

5   When the figure is dressed, bend the legs into a sitting position and secure her so that she looks as though she is on the chair. Make a small oval of dough for the baby's body and attach a little ball of dough at one end for the head. Add a tiny nose and wrap the baby in a shawl made by cutting out a circle of rolled-out dough with the fluted cutter. Mark a faint pattern on the shawl with the pointed end of a modelling tool. Arrange the baby in Mary's arms and attach some hair made by extruding dough through a clay gun.

6   Cut a long strip of thinly rolled dough measuring 17.5×6.5cm ($7 \times 2\frac{1}{2}$in). Mark the middle and use this point as a guide for cutting a curve along one side. The strip should still be 6.5cm ($2\frac{1}{2}$in) wide at the ends, but the curve should taper its width to only 4cm ($1\frac{1}{2}$in) in the middle. Drape this strip over Mary's head, making folds in the ends.

7   Make legs, arms and a body for Joseph, see page 13. Set the arms aside. Cut a triangle from thinly rolled dough, measuring 9cm ($3\frac{1}{2}$in) across the base and 12.5cm (5in) along the sides. Cut 12mm ($\frac{1}{2}$in) off the apex of the triangle to shape the neck of the robe. Fit the dough around Joseph with the cut off top

around his neck. Secure Joseph beside Mary, draping any spare dough in his robe.

8   Fix two thin ropes around Joseph's wrists to make cuffs. Fix the arms onto the body, so that one is around Mary and the other rests across Joseph's body. Flatten a thin rope of dough around the neck of Joseph's robe and indent it with a retracted ballpoint pen. Make a round ball of dough for Joseph's head and add a wedge-shaped nose. Use the clay gun to make a beard and hair for Joseph. Shape a slightly droopy moustache on his face.

9   To make the sheep, roll four thin, 4cm ($1\frac{1}{2}$in) long ropes and make a little cut in the middle of one end of each. Arrange these in pairs on the stable base, next to Mary. Cover the tops of the legs with a flattened oval of dough for the body, supporting it on a small pad of foil to prevent it falling back on the baking tray. Model a small ball of dough into a slightly pointed sheep's face and rest it on Mary's cloak, looking at the baby. Flatten two very small balls of dough into cupped ears with the rounded end of a modelling tool. Fix these on the sheep.

10   Make dozens of tiny ropes and roll them up into curls. Secure them to cover the top of the sheep's head and all the body. Secure a few more curls together to make a tail.

11   Roll two pencil-thin ropes and make feet at one end, see page 13. Lay these on the thatched roof. Cut out a triangle of rolled-out dough with a 10cm (4in) base and sides. Still keeping the triangle in shape, tuck the sides under and lay it over the legs with the feet protruding to make the angel's robe.

12   Make a round ball of dough for the head and attach it to the pointed end of the robe. Make a trumpet by rolling out a thin 4cm ($1\frac{1}{2}$in) rope which is slightly thicker at one end. Widen the thick end into a trumpet shape with the rounded end of a modelling

tool. Secure the thin end of the trumpet against the angel's face and lay the rest along the left-hand column of the stable.

13 Make hands and arms, and attach cuffs made from very small ropes; secure the arms to the robe. Place the hands on the trumpet. Make a nose from a tiny ball of dough and attach it above the trumpet. Make hair from sieved dough, see page 13.

14 To make wings, cut out two triangles from thinly rolled dough, measuring 4cm (1½in) across each base and 5cm (2in) along the sides. Lay these beside each other, base down, then trim off the outside corner of each. Use a sharp knife to cut pointed shapes into the outer edges. Decorate the points with the retracted ballpoint pen. Place the wings on the angel with the straight sides innermost and the tops of the triangles close to the head.

15 Roll out some dough to 6mm (¼in) and use the daisy cutter to make a star. Secure this firmly to the straw overhanging the left-hand side of the roof. Secure a hanging hook into each side of the roof and brush the roof, columns and base with egg glaze. Bake at 145°C (290°F/Gas 1½) for about 3 hours.

Painting and Finishing

● Mix up flesh colour and paint the faces and hands of all the figures, also Joseph's feet, see page 42. Paint Mary with her eyes closed, looking down at the baby. Add a little Red Ochre to white to make the deep pink of Mary's dress. Add white to Ultramarine to mix the colour of her cloak.

Paint Joseph's robe in pure Burnt Sienna and leave to dry. Use a rigger brush to paint on wide stripes with diluted Yellow Ochre. Mix Cadmium Yellow and Ultramarine to make a dull green and paint more stripes.

Make up watery Permanent White and paint the baby's shawl and angel's robe and

wings. While the wings are wet, blend first a little watery Ultramarine, then some thin Cadmium Red into their edges. Paint the sheep's wool with the same watery white, but do not worry too much about getting paint into all the nooks and crannies, as leaving some dough bare will give the coat depth.

Use pure Jet Black to paint shoes on Joseph's feet and the face and legs of the sheep. When the sheep is quite dry, add pale blue eyes and tint the insides of the ears with watery Cadmium Red. Finally, use Gold to paint the star and angel's trumpet, then paint a design along the hem of the robe and the decoration on the wings. Add a few golden highlights on the hair. Trim the edge of Mary's cloak with Gold and paint a circle and dot pattern over the outside.

Christmas Tree Angel, *page 109.*

TABLE DECORATIONS

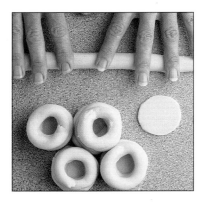

Coiling the rope in layers to make the candle holders.

The coils are assembled in the ring of twisted dough, with the taller one in the middle.

Dough is an ideal medium for making a table centrepiece. You can be as simple or as lavish as you like and, unlike a floral decoration, it will last for years. This section gives ideas for Easter and Christmas table decorations, and also includes instructions for making napkin holders and place names.

·EASTER CENTREPIECE·

$1\frac{1}{4}$ quantities Basic Dough, see page 10
5cm (2in) round cutter
fresh primrose leaf
nail scissors
primrose cutter
wooden skewer
daffodil cutters
small leaf cutter
blossom plunger cutter • candles

1   Make a 55cm (22in) twist from one-third of the dough, see page 12. Arrange this in a ring on a baking sheet and join the ends together with a little water.

2   Roll out some dough to 6mm ($\frac{1}{4}$in) thick and cut out seven 5cm (2in) circles. Dampen the edge of one circle. Roll out a pencil-thin rope about 45cm (18in) long, see page 11, and coil it around the edge of the dampened dough circle. Coil the rope up in layers, dampening each layer of rope, to build up a cylindrical candle holder. Complete five more candle holders in the same way, making the last one a little taller by rolling a slightly longer rope. Place the taller candle holder in the middle of

the dough ring and fit the others around it, damping them a little where they touch each other and where they touch the outer ring of dough.

3   Roll out some dough slightly thinner than before and press the primrose leaf into it, veined side down. Carefully lift the leaf off the dough and use the nail scissors to cut out the leaf impression in the dough. Make three more leaves and arrange them evenly around the edge of the twisted ring.

4   Cut out 20 primroses and arrange them in groups of five on the twist, close to the leaves. Indent the centre of each flower with the wooden skewer. Using the daffodil cutters, model four daffodils directly on the twist, arranging them in pairs on opposite sides of the ring, see page 17.

5   Make six violets, see page 16, and arrange these in groups of three on the ring. Cut out six small leaves and arrange them around the groups of violets. Cut out several small blossoms and fix them around the ring, remembering to fix one to the end of each coil.

6   Finally, flour the end of a candle and wobble it around in each candle holder to ensure that there will be plenty of room for the candles once the ring has been baked. The dough tends to shrink a little during cooking so you may find that you have to shave the ends off your candles before arranging them in the holder. Bake at 145°C (290°F/Gas $1\frac{1}{2}$) for about $3\frac{1}{2}$ hours.

Easter Centrepiece

Painting and Finishing

● Make a watery mix of Olive Green and a little Lemon Yellow and wash this over the primrose leaves. Add a little Permanent White to Lemon Yellow to paint the centres of the primroses. When dry, paint the centres with the same green mix as the leaves.

Use pure Golden Yellow for the outer petals of the daffodils and add a little Rose Madder to make the colour for the trumpets. Add a little more Rose Madder and paint the edges of the trumpets while the first coat is still damp. Ring the centres of the primroses with the same colour.

Paint the violets with pure Spectrum Violet and the violet leaves with Olive Green with a touch of Ultramarine added.

Add a little Ultramarine to Permanent White to paint the forget-me-knots. Blush the petals with a touch of Rose Madder and white while still wet.

· CHRISTMAS ·
PLACE NAMES

These salt-dough place names do not take much longer to make than a batch of mince pies but, if you pack them away carefully, they will last far longer.

$\frac{3}{4}$ quantity Basic Dough, see page 10
5cm (2in) fluted round cutter
cocktail stick (toothpick)
thin plastic drinking straw
very small holly leaf cutter
Egg Glaze, see page 11
1.5m (62in) narrow red ribbon
fast-drying glue

1   Roll out about a third of the dough to 6mm ($\frac{1}{4}$in) thick and cut out six 6.5 × 12mm ($2\frac{1}{2}$ × $\frac{1}{2}$in) strips; set these aside.

2   Roll out some fresh dough to 3mm ($\frac{1}{8}$in) thick and cut out six fluted circles. Frill the edges of the circles with a cocktail stick (toothpick), see page 14, leaving their centres complete. Cut a third from each frilled circle and set these pieces aside. Use a thin plastic drinking straw to make ribbon eyelet holes at regular intervals about 12mm ($\frac{1}{2}$in) in from the frilled edge of the remaining pieces.

3   Lay the large pieces on a baking tray and fix one of the strips, side on, along the unfrilled edge of each of them. Coat these with egg glaze and bake them at 145°C (290°F/Gas $1\frac{1}{2}$) for about 30 minutes or until firm.

4   While the first pieces are baking, make similar eyelet holes in the remaining sections and set them aside with the rest of the dough; cover with a lightly dampened cloth.

5   Stand the baked pieces up so that the frilled part stands up like a shell at the back. Roll six very thin ropes and use these to stick the smaller frilled pieces on top of the front of the strips. Brush the front and the back of the larger frilled pieces with egg glaze.

6   Roll out some dough thinly and cut out twelve very small holly leaves. Arrange these in pairs on the fronts of all the holders and add a few very small balls of dough for berries.

7   Return the holders to the oven, standing them upright, and bake for about 1 hour at the same temperature. If the base of the holder has risen or become slightly puffy during the first baking, lay a metal knife handle across it during the second cooking.

Painting and Finishing

● Paint the holly leaves with pure Olive Green and allow to dry. Then paint the edges of the frills, the holly berries and some lining on the base in Spectrum Red. Varnish in the usual way and allow to dry.

Start threading a piece of ribbon from each end of the back frill on one of the holders. Leave the tails of the ribbon at the back of the holder and thread the pieces of ribbon through the eyelets until they meet in the middle. Tie the ends into a small bow at the front and trim off any excess ribbon. Turn to the back of the holder and trim the ribbon tails, leaving just enough to secure them in place with a dab of fast-drying glue. Finish all the holders in the same way.

· CHRISTMAS · NAPKIN RINGS

These Christmas napkin rings make a charming, rustic addition to the table, particularly if you make matching place names and bowls.

4 cardboard cylinders from kitchen paper or toilet rolls
cooking foil
$\frac{3}{4}$ quantity Basic Dough, see page 10
plastic ruler
5cm (2in) fluted round cutter
cocktail stick (toothpick)
2.5cm (1in) round cutter
small holly leaf cutter
thin plastic drinking straw
Egg Glaze, see page 11
rigger brush
1m (40in) narrow red ribbon
fast-drying glue

1 Cover the cardboard cylinders with cooking foil and set them aside. Roll out half the dough to 6mm ($\frac{1}{4}$in) thick; using a well-floured ruler and a sharp knife cut four 2.5cm (1in) wide strips long enough to fit around the cylinders. Wrap the strips around the cylinders and fix the ends together with a little water. Flour the joins lightly in case they

Christmas Place Names and Christmas Napkin Rings

117

Fixing strips on the unfrilled side of a large piece.

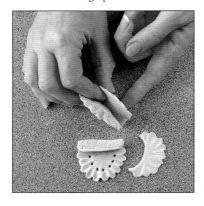

Fixing the smaller frilled section on the baked pieces.

CRAFT TIP

Napkin rings are a law unto themselves and no two ever seem to turn out exactly alike or even, sometimes, precisely as you planned, but it really does not matter, they always look wonderful on the table.

---

are damp and then stand the cylinders and rings, join downwards, on a baking tray.

2 Roll out some more dough to 3mm ($\frac{1}{8}$ in) thick and cut out four circles with the fluted cutter. Frill the edges of the circles with a cocktail stick (toothpick), see page 14, and then remove the middle of each with the small round cutter to make rings.

3 Cut the rings in half and then fix two halves facing each other, on either side of the top of each napkin ring. If the frills are likely to fall back, prop them up with foil.

4 Cut out twelve holly leaves and arrange these in groups of three on top of each ring, adding a few small balls of dough for berries. Starting on either side of the holly, use a thin drinking straw to make two or three holes around the sides of the rings; these will be used for threading ribbon.

5 Paint the rings, excluding the holly, with egg glaze and bake at 145°C (290°F/Gas 1$\frac{1}{2}$) for about 1$\frac{1}{2}$ hours.

Painting and Finishing

● Paint all the leaves with Olive Green and leave to dry. Paint the berries and the edge of the frill with Spectrum Red. Use a rigger brush to paint a single red line around each of the rings on either side of the ribbon holes.

Varnish in the usual way; you may like to use yacht varnish as the napkin rings could come into contact with liquid. When the varnish is dry, thread the ribbon through the holes and glue the ends neatly on the inside.

FESTIVE TABLE ·CENTREPIECE·

By the time the food has been set on the festive dinner table, there is not very much room for a centrepiece and many of my more extravagant efforts have ended up on the sideboard or – worse still – under it.

hand cream
$\frac{1}{2}$ *quantity Bread Dough, see page 10*
Cadmium Red gouache or water colour paint
waxed paper
large and medium rose leaf cutters
cling film (plastic wrap)
modelling tool
small black stamens
Olive Green gouache or water colour paint
holly leaf cutter
primrose cutter
piece of tree bark, about 20cm (8in) long
gold spray paint
sauce bottle top
fast-drying glue
Lemon Yellow gouache or water colour paint
Jet Black gouache or water colour paint
small yellow stamens
Linden Green gouache or water colour paint
spirit-based clear gloss acrylic varnish
candle
50cm (20in) wide green ribbon

1 Rub hand cream into your hands, then take a piece of bread dough about the size of a large walnut, and colour it with Cadmium Red paint, see page 11. Flatten the dough into a round and place it between two pieces of waxed paper, then gently roll it out thinly.
2 Use the larger of the two rose leaf cutters to cut out fourteen poinsettia bracts or petals. Knead the scraps of dough together and roll

Festive Table Centrepiece

Rolling a modelling tool on a bract to give it a slightly undulating edge.

Gluing the poinsettia bracts onto the bark.

them out again; cut out ten more bracts with the smaller rose leaf cutter. Gather up the scraps again and wrap them in cling film.

3 Rub more hand cream onto your hands and on the rounded end of a modelling tool. Lay one of the bracts in the palm of your hand and carefully roll the rounded end of the modelling tool along each side of it to stretch the dough slightly and give the bract slightly undulating edges. Repeat with the remaining bracts and set them aside on a piece of waxed paper to dry.

4 Roll the remaining red dough into eight small balls to represent holly berries. Trim most of the stalk from one of the black stamens and fix it into one berry; repeat with the other berries, then set them aside to dry with the leaves.

5 Take a slightly larger piece of white dough than before and colour it with Olive Green paint, see page 11. Roll this out between waxed paper, then cut out eight leaves with the large rose cutter and seven holly leaves. Roll the edges of the rose leaves as before and set these and the holly leaves aside to dry.

6 Roll out a small piece of the white dough as before and use the primrose cutter to cut out five Christmas roses. Rub more hand cream into your hands and on the rounded end of the modelling tool. Lay a flower in the palm of your hand and gently press and roll each of the petals with the modelling tool before finally pressing it in the middle so that it cups slightly. Repeat with the remaining flowers, then set them aside on waxed paper to dry. Finally, make about twenty very small white balls and leave these to dry.

Painting and Finishing

● Make sure that the piece of bark is clean and dry, and then spray it sparsely with gold paint, so that it receives just a dusting of gold,

allowing the wood to show through. Wash and dry the sauce bottle top and give that a solid coat of gold. Leave both until completely dry.

Use fast-drying glue to fix the sauce bottle top upside down on the bark to act as a candle holder.

Paint the poinsettia petals with Cadmium Red and the leaves with a mixture of Olive Green and Lemon Yellow. Allow these to dry before painting some veins on the leaves with pure Olive Green. Paint the holly leaves with pure Olive Green and the holly berries with Cadmium Red. Add a touch of Jet Black to the stamens when the berries are dry.

Paint the Christmas roses white and allow these to dry, then glue four or five yellow stamen heads into the middle of each flower. When the glue has dried, paint some watery Linden Green on and around the stamens, and blend this into the white with a clean damp brush. Finish the stamens by brushing some pure Linden Green over their tops.

Glue seven of the larger poinsettia bracts, overlapping each other slightly, to form a circle on the bark and with part of the circle leaning up against the candle holder.

Fix five small bracts inside the larger ones so that they overlap in a similar way to form the centre of the flower. Glue ten small balls into the middle of the flower and fix three or four leaves behind the outer bracts.

Make a second arrangement with the remainder of the poinsettia bracts and leaves, and position this so that it also obscures the sides of the candle holder. Fill the centre with the remaining little balls.

Arrange five holly leaves together so that some lean against the candle holder and some lay on the bark. Then position five holly berries in the centre of the group. Lay the remaining holly leaves and berries close to the second poinsettia and dot the Christmas roses around singly and in pairs to balance the arrangement.

When all the flowers are in place and the glue is dry, give all the dough pieces a coat of spirit-based acrylic varnish and allow this to dry thoroughly.

Finally, fix the candle into the holder and add a bow of green ribbon; glue this at one end of the arrangement close to the candle.

·THANKSGIVING SHEAF·

The Thanksgiving sheaf is made to a traditional design with origins in the mists of time, probably as far back as pagan times, when bread was often baked in ritual shapes and offered to the gods in the hope of a good harvest. Little is known about the early artistic history of bread and we are not sure when a more durable, but inedible, recipe for dough was made, so that the bakers' efforts would survive to become cherished ornaments.

$1\frac{1}{2}$ quantities Basic Dough, see page 10
Egg Glaze, see page 11
15cm (6in) saucer
nail scissors • modelling tool
very fine floristry wire
cocktail stick (toothpick)
1 hairpin
1m (40in) orange ribbon

1   Roll out about a quarter of the dough to 6mm ($\frac{1}{4}$in) thick. Using the saucer as a template, cut out a circle of dough and place it at one end of a baking tray. Cut a 12.5 × 7.5cm (5 × 3in) rectangle of dough and fix this on the circle so that it overlaps by about 12mm ($\frac{1}{2}$in) to resemble a lollipop with a fat stick.

2   Take a handful of dough and roll out a 30cm (12in) long pencil-thin rope, leaving 5cm (2in) at one end about twice as thick.

Lay this down the middle of the lollipop shape so that it overhangs by about 2.5cm (1in) at the fat end and 6mm ($\frac{1}{4}$in) at the thin end.

3   Use scissors to make a row of nicks around the base of the fat end to represent an ear of corn. Snip a second row behind the first and continue until the whole ear of corn is complete. Make 14 more ears of corn and arrange them symmetrically on either side of the first one to completely cover the base. Some of the circle will still be showing, but this will be covered by the next layer of corn.

Thanksgiving Sheaf

Making ears of corn.

121

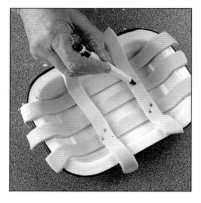

Making dots to represent nails on the strips of dough.

CRAFT TIP

The inside of a pie dish acts as a mould to make the hen house for this mother and her chicks. The idea can also be adapted for other projects, where you wish to give the impression that the figures are inside their house, looking out.

4   Make 15 more ears of corn, this time making them 22.5cm (9in) long. Pile these on top of the first layer so that their tops are about 4cm (1½in) lower and with some of their heads drooping down to cover the rest of the circle. When all the stalks are in place and all the heads are nicked, pinch the dough in as though the corn is bound in a sheaf.

5   To make the body of the mouse, mould a small handful of dough into a pear shape. Fix this on the ears of corn with a little water. Make two ears by indenting two small balls of dough with the round end of a modelling tool. Arrange these on top of the mouse's head and mark the eyes with a cocktail stick (toothpick). Cut the floristry wire into six short lengths and stick three of them into the dough on either side of his nose. Finally, roll a thin tapering tail of dough and arrange it so that it curls out across the dough behind the mouse.

6   Fix the hairpin firmly in the top so that most of it is embedded in the dough. Paint the sheaf all over with egg glaze. Bake at 145°C (290°F/Gas 1½) for 3 to 4 hours, brushing with more glaze once or twice for a rich colour.

Painting and Finishing

●   Make up some watery Alizarin and wash it onto the mouse's tail, ears and nose. Then use Jet Black to mark his eyes and whiskers. Varnish and decorate with a ribbon when dry.

· MOTHER HEN ·

20 × 15cm (8 × 6in) pie dish
vegetable oil
¾ quantity Basic Dough, see page 10
plastic ruler
retracted ballpoint pen
garlic press or clay gun
rose petal cutter
modelling tool
small bird cutter
cocktail stick (toothpick)
Egg Glaze, see page 11
poppy seeds
50cm (20in) yellow ribbon

1   Thoroughly coat the inside and the lip of the pie dish with oil and put it to one side. Roll out about a third of the dough to 6mm (¼in) thick. Then use a well-floured plastic ruler and a sharp knife to cut three strips measuring about 22.5 × 2cm (9 × ¾in). Lay these lengthways, evenly spaced, along the bottom of the dish so that they reach up the sides with their ends resting on the lip.

2   Cut two 17.5 × 2cm (7 × ¾in) strips and lay them at right angles over the first strips. Dab a little water where the two sets of strips cross and then mark a couple of dots on the junctions to represent nails.

3   Take a good handful of dough and roll a finger-thick 70cm (28in) long rope. Dampen the ends of all the strips and then, starting at one corner, fit the roll around the top of the pie dish. Flatten the roll slightly with your fingers and make 'nail' marks with the ballpoint pen wherever it crosses the end of a strip.

4   From now on, as you work, prop up the pie dish slightly on one long side, so that you can get a better idea of what the design will look like when it is finished and hanging on the wall. Use the clay gun or garlic press to

Mother Hen

*Using a small metal tube to mark
feather-like shapes on the bird's chest.*

build up a good nest of 'straw' in the bottom half of the dish. The straw should stretch from side to side and reach up about as far as the middle strip.

5   Model a small handful of dough into a tear-drop shape for the hen's body. Make a few feather-like shapes on the chest and back of the body by using a small metal tube, like the cap of an eyebrow pencil or something similar, to indent the dough at an angle while lifting it slightly. This will create small flaps of dough that resemble feathers.

6   To make the wings, roll out a small amount of dough thinly and cut out two leaves with the rose leaf cutter. Starting close to the pointed ends, cut two notches along one side of each leaf. Fix these on the hen's body, rounded ends to the front and the notched sides uppermost.

7   Sit the hen in the straw, then model an oval shape for the head. Pull a small, pointed piece of dough out at one end of the oval to represent a beak and then fix the head onto the body, so that she appears to be looking back over her shoulder.

8   Flatten four small balls of dough and arrange these in a line along the top of the hen's head to represent her comb. Flatten another ball of dough, cut it in half and fix it under her chin.

9   Mould three small pear-shaped pieces of dough for the chicks and pinch the narrow ends into little tails. Make three small balls for heads and pull a small pointed piece of dough out on one side of each for a beak.

10   Fix the heads onto the bodies and place two chicks in the straw behind the mother hen, and one in front of her. Use a cocktail stick (toothpick) to mark eyes on the hen and her chicks.

11   Roll a fairly small ball of dough and hollow out the middle with the rounded end of a modelling tool to make a small bowl shape. Place this in the straw towards the back of the dish.

12   Use the small bird cutter to indent a design on the long sides of the rim, marking a bird between each set of nails.

13   Model 24 small eggs and place two of these just under the hen. Arrange the rest in pairs to complete the decoration on the rim.

14   Paint the dish with the egg glaze, but do not paint the hen, chicks and bowl. Drip a little glaze into the bottom of the bowl and sprinkle some poppy seeds onto it. Bake at 145°C (290°F/Gas 1½) for about 2 hours.

Painting and Finishing

● Mix a little white into some Burnt Sienna to make a warm light brown. Paint the hen with this and before it has a chance to dry, add a little more white to the mixture and paint little arcs of colour onto her chest feathers.

Use the same colour to suggest a double line of feathers on either side of her face and to draw a couple of curving lines under her eyes. Use Jet Black to accentuate her eyes and to paint some feathery shapes on the top half of her back and the rounded end of her wings. Add a line of Cadmium Red dots to the feather patterns on her back and wing, and use the same colour to paint the comb and chin piece.

Use some pure Lemon Yellow to paint the beak and add a little white to this to get the colour for the chicks. While the pale yellow is still damp on the chicks, add a little watery Cadmium Red to their cheeks. Add a tiny speck of red to the pale yellow to get a pale orange for their little beaks. Dot their eyes with Jet Black and draw two curved lines in pale brown on their sides to suggest wings. Paint the decorative birds on the rim of the dish in the same way.

Mix some Ultramarine and white together to make the pale blue for the bowl and paint this carefully so as not to get paint on the poppy seeds. When the bowl is quite dry, decorate the rim and sides with two slightly darker blue lines. Finally, paint all the eggs white.

Varnish in the usual way and allow to dry. Loop a piece of yellow ribbon loosely around the two strips at the rear of the hen house. Tie the ends in a firm bow at the front and hang the house by the slack ribbon at the back.

· CANDELABRA ·

1¼ quantities Basic Dough see page 10
retracted ballpoint pen
cocktail stick (toothpick)
modelling tool
ivy leaf cutter
2 or 3 fine floristry wires
2 Hanging Hooks, see page 17
gold spray paint
9 small white candles
clear gloss polyurethane varnish

1 Roll about a quarter of the dough into a fairly thick 34cm (13½in) long rope. Lay this horizontally on a baking tray and lightly mark the middle point on the rope.

2 Make a second, slightly thicker, 10cm (4in) long rope and butt it up to the middle of the first one at right angles. Fix the ropes together with a little water.

3 Make three, short, finger-thick ropes, 6.5cm (2½in), 7.5cm (3in), and 10cm (4in) long. Fix these horizontally, in order of size so that they form a pedestal, at the base of the vertical rope.

4 Make two pencil-thin 20cm (8in) ropes. Take one of these and trim one end diagonally before fixing it to the upright column about 5cm (2in) down from the intersection with the horizontal rope. Lay the rest of the rope across one of the corners made by the intersection and fix it 5cm (2in) along the horizontal bar, then coil the remainder of the rope back on itself. Secure the coil in position to resemble an ornamental bracket. Use the

second 20cm (8in) rope to make a similar bracket for the other side.

5 Make a very thin rope and fix it around the join between the top rope of the pedestal and the upright column.

Decorate the three ropes that make the pedestal with stars of David and marks made with the retracted ballpoint pen. I have also added a few little balls of dough and indented their middles with the cocktail stick.

6 Make ten walnut-sized balls of dough. Flatten one of these slightly, then fix it on top of the horizontal rope, in the middle.

7 Use the rounded end of a modelling tool to hollow out the other nine balls so that they resemble little round pots. Place one of these on top of the centre ball and fix the others evenly along the horizontal rope so that there are four on either side.

8 Roll nine very thin ropes, about 7.5cm (3in) long, and fix one of these around the top of each pot to make a lip. The pots should stay open while they are baking, but if you are concerned that they might collapse inwards, prop them open with wads of cooking foil. Decorate the centre pot with a line of marks made using the retracted ballpoint pen and use the cocktail stick (toothpick) to make similar marks on the others.

9 Roll out half of the remaining dough to 3mm (⅛in) thick and cut out about 20 ivy leaves. Mark a central vein on the leaves and put them to one side while you roll several dozen little balls to represent grapes. Build up bunches of grapes, with leaves attached, down the column and along the cross bar.

10 Cut some floristry wire into 5cm (2in) lengths and wind these around a pencil to make tendrils. Push one end of these into the dough where you have a bunch of leaves and grapes.

11 Push a hanging hook into the back of each of the end pots and bake for about 3 hours at 145°C (290°F/Gas 1½).

Attaching an ornamental bracket.

CRAFT TIP

Most candelabras or menorahs for Chanukah are metal, so you could paint this one silver or gold, but as it is richly ornamented I thought it would look more interesting and exciting with a verdigris finish. Please remind the family that you must not light the candles on this plaque.

Candelabra

Painting and Finishing

● Give the menorah two or three thin coats of gold paint. When completely dry, mix Viridian and, working quickly, completely cover the gold with this colour. While damp blend a mixture of white and Viridian into some areas: mainly in the nooks and crannies around the pots, and between the leaves and grapes, but do not overdo this. When the paint is almost dry, take a soft, lint-free cloth and rub some of it away to reveal the gold.

When you are satisfied with the effect, allow the paint to dry and add a coat of clear gloss polyurethane varnish. The gold will gleam if you apply two or three coats of varnish; leave 24 hours between applications.

Shave the bottoms off the little candles and arrange them in the holders.

ROMANTIC MESSAGES

Make the one you love a very special personal gift. You can choose from the models of cheeky cherubs, pretty hearts and loving doves for a truly romantic message.

·LOVE BIRDS HEART·

1 quantity Basic Dough, see page 10
large bird cutter
old retractable ballpoint pen
leaf cutters • rose cutters
blossom plunger cutter
Hanging Hook, see page 17

1 Make a fairly substantial twist from slightly more than half the dough, see page 12. Form this into a heart shape on a baking sheet. Mitre the ends of the dough and join them to a point where the heart dips at the top.

2 Roll out some dough to 6mm ($\frac{1}{4}$in) thick and cut out four birds. Neatly cut off the wings from two birds. Notch the ends of these wings and those on the two complete birds to represent feathers. Notch both tails in the same way. Attach the loose wings on top of the wings of the birds, fixing them at a slight angle. Use the back of your knife to make a slight indentation in the beak and the old pen to mark the eyes. Arrange the birds facing each other inside the heart, so that their beaks are just touching and their bodies can be fixed to the sides of the heart. Try to tilt the wings up to fix them to the dip in the heart.

3 Cut four large leaves from some rolled dough and arrange these on either side of the join at the top of the heart. Make one full rose, one smaller rose without the final four petals and one rosebud, see page 15, then arrange these over the leaves to completely cover the join. Cut two smaller leaves and place these back to back on the point of the heart. Roll out some dough to make a thin, large bow with 10cm (4in) trailing ribbons, see page 13. Arrange this under the beaks of the birds with the ends trailing over the edges of the heart.

4 Cut out about 24 small blossoms. Use six to make a posy on the small leaves at the bottom of the heart, then fix the remainder around the roses and ribbon. Fit the hanging hook in the dip of the heart and bake at 145°C (290°F/Gas 1$\frac{1}{2}$) for about 2 hours.

Painting and Finishing

● Paint the leaves with watery Olive Green leaving a few random patches bare. While still wet, add a little thin Alizarin Crimson to the patches and blend with a clean damp brush. Paint the roses with pure Alizarin Crimson. Add very little Ultramarine to Permanent White to make a pale blue for the forget-me-knots. Add a little pink, made from Alizarin and white, to the forget-me-knots while the blue is still damp.

   Paint the birds with Permanent White and add some pink and blue while still damp. Blend these colours very carefully with a damp clean brush. Paint the ribbon with pale

Love Birds Heart
Making the birds: two birds are cut but only the wings are used from the second shape.

CRAFT TIP

If you want to write a romantic message on the ribbon, use either a very fine brush or a fine waterproof felt-tipped pen.

Entwined Hearts

Cutting the dough to make a neat join at the top of the heart.

blue and edge with Gold. Decorate the edges of the birds' wings and tails with gold. Use yellow to paint the birds' beaks and mix with Alizarin for the eyes; alternatively, paint both Gold.

·ENTWINED HEARTS·

¾ quantity Basic Dough, see page 10
large bird cutter
modelling tool
3 Hanging Hooks, see page 17
large initial cutters, optional
medium leaf cutter
rose cutters
blossom plunger cutter
small heart cutter
old retractable ballpoint pen

1 Roll out half the dough to 6mm ($\frac{1}{2}$in) thick. Cut out two birds, then trim the wings off one bird and use to make a bird following the instructions for Love Birds Heart, see page 127. Use the modelling tool to make a hole in the bottom of the bird and fix a hanging hook in the top.

2 Roll out two pencil-thin, 25cm (10in) long ropes of dough and shape these into hearts on a baking sheet. Join the dough in the dip at the top of each heart. Move the hearts so that one just overlaps the other on one corner.

3 Cut out the chosen initials and fix them inside the hearts. Alternatively, the initials can be made from slightly flattened, thin ropes of dough.

4 Cut out four leaves, mark veins on them, then arrange them in pairs on either side of the joins at the top of the hearts. Place a small rose, see page 15, in the middle of each pair.

5 Cut out several blossoms, arrange three of these on each initial and group the others

around the roses. Indent a pattern around the hearts using the heart cutter and old pen, then place a hanging hook in the dip of each heart.

6 Bake at 145°C (290°F/Gas 1$\frac{1}{2}$) for 1 hour. Check that the bird is not overbaking and remove it, if necessary, then continue to bake the hearts for a further 30 minutes.

Painting and Finishing

● Paint the leaves with thin Olive Green and the roses with pure Rose Madder. Make a pool of Ultramarine mixed with white and another of Rose Madder mixed with white. Using both thinly, wash the bird in blue adding a gentle blush of pink here and there while the blue is wet.

Thicken the blue slightly and paint the blossoms, adding a touch of pink too. Use pink and blue to paint the heart and dot pattern. Paint a few small green leaves around the blue flowers on the initials. Finish by lining the initials and dots with Gold and by touching the bird's eye, beak, and feathers with a little Gold.

Varnish and allow to dry. Loop satin ribbon through the hole in the bird and the hooks in the hearts. Fix with a stitch of blue cotton or glue.

Love Birds Heart

Entwined Hearts, page 128

130

VALENTINE'S DAY
· MIRROR ·

$\frac{3}{4}$ quantity Basic Dough, see page 10
15cm (6in) saucer
10cm (4in) and 2.5cm (1in) round cutters
5cm (2in) fluted round cutter
cocktail stick (toothpick)
large heart crimper
medium rose leaf cutter
primrose cutter
Hanging Hook, see page 17
2–3 stamens
12.5cm (5in) square mirror tile or small mirror
strong glue or hot glue gun

1   Roll out half the dough to 6mm ($\frac{1}{4}$in) thick. Using the saucer as a guide, cut a circle from the rolled-out dough, then use the 10cm (4in) cutter to cut out the middle of the circle. Place the ring of dough on a baking tray.

2   Roll out some more dough to 3mm ($\frac{1}{8}$in) thick. Cut out about 22 fluted circles with the 5cm (2in) cutter. Then frill the edges of each circle, page 14, repeatedly flouring the cocktail stick. Cut the circles in half and attach about 11 halves to the outside of the large ring so that the frilled curves form a scalloped edge around the outside. Attach the remaining semi-circles in a ring on top of and just inside the first ones. Arrange the second row so that the scallops alternate with the first set.

3   Make a 45cm (18in) long pencil-thick rope of dough. Press this around the dampened inside edge of the upper frill so that it is slightly flattened and then use the crimper to decorate the rope of dough with hearts.

4   Model a plump heart from a walnut-sized piece of dough, making the notch at the top with the back of a knife. Fix this onto the heart border at the top of the mirror frame. Model

two doves, see page 15, and arrange them slightly to the right of the heart.

5   Using the rose leaf cutter, cut out and vein seven leaves, see page 16. Place six leaves, in two groups of three, opposite the doves and at the bottom of the frame. Fit the last leaf in between the heart and the doves.

6   Use the 2.5cm (1in) circular cutter to make one large and three smaller roses, see page 15. Place one small rose on the single leaf and the other two side-by-side on the three leaves on the side of the frame. Fix the large rose in the middle of the three leaves at the bottom of the frame. Using the same cutter, make four rose-buds, see page 15, and tuck one of these behind the two small roses. Arrange the other three rosebuds around the single large rose.

7   Cut out three dog roses with the primrose cutter and slightly cup the petals, see page 16. Place two of these close to the doves and the other one near the heart. Arrange three shortened stamens in the centre of each dog-rose.

8   Roll two very thin, short ropes of dough and make these into rings to represent wedding rings. Overlap the rings between the doves.

9   Decorate the space between the objects and below the border with dozens of little balls of dough in a variety of sizes, all pierced with the sharp end of a modelling tool. Push a hanging hook behind the lace and the large heart; because this is a heavy item use a whole hook. Bake at 145°C (290°F/Gas 1$\frac{1}{2}$) for about 2 hours.

Painting and Finishing

● Dampen the frill around the edge of the mirror with a clean brush dipped in water, then paint on some slightly diluted Permanent White. The white paint on the frill should be opaque but not thick.

CRAFT TIP

Using dough to make a frame for a mirror does not have to be restricted to Valentine's day. This design can easily be adapted for Christmas by changing the doves to robins, the heart to a bow and the flowers to holly or Christmas roses. If you are feeling more adventurous, you could change the shape completely and decorate it with just about anything. I often make nautical frames, with sea-shells, mermaids and fishes. It is actually possible to bake the mirror into the dough (as for the china beads on the Engagement Bowl, see page 135) but as it must never be placed directly on a baking tray and will crack unless it is evenly supported on a bed of dough, it is far safer to glue the mirror on after the frame is baked.

Putting on the first row of frilled semi-circles.

Decorating the inner rim with hearts.

Remember always to paint and varnish the back of any part of the design that overlaps the middle of a mirror as it will be reflected in the glass.

Paint the doves and the dog roses with the same mixture, then blush them with a little watery Rose Madder on the petal edges and also on the fronts, tails and the wings of the doves. Use well-diluted Ultramarine to tip the doves' tails and wings.

Paint each of the small hearts on the border with the thin Rose Madder. Paint the leaves with some thin Olive Green and variegate them slightly with some of the thin Rose Madder.

Thicken the Rose Madder by adding some fresh paint and use this to paint the roses, rosebuds and the big heart. Mark the doves' eyes with little specks of Ultramarine. Paint their beaks and the dog rose stamens with orange, made by mixing Rose Madder and Lemon Yellow.

Trim the edges of the frills, the doves' wings and their tails with some slightly diluted gold paint. Paint the wedding rings gold.

Finally, I have worked a little diluted gold into the tips and around the edges of the leaves to give a more Victorian look – make sure that you leave it at that . . . it is easy to run amuck when armed with gold on a brush and end up with a very garish model!

When the paint is dry, varnish the dough in the usual way, applying a couple of coats to the back. This is to ensure that the dough does not absorb the glue and prevent the mirror from bonding to it. When the varnish is completely dry, fix the mirror to the back of the frame using strong glue. If you use a hot glue gun, place the glue on the back of the frame and allow it to cool for a few seconds before attaching the mirror.

· CHERUBS AND HEARTS ·

It was the Victorians who really made a great romantic festival out of Saint Valentine's day and, as usual, they didn't hold back.

Victorian Valentine cards showed cherubs carrying baskets full of quivering red hearts or staggering under overflowing cornucopias of them, while others were often depicted understandably exhausted and asleep on huge piles of broken hearts. Some cherubs had an easier time of it admittedly and were simply put in charge of flocks of doves or writing and delivering love letters, but that still left the gathering of roses, lace and butterflies to worry about. February 14th was a hectic time for the poor old Victorian cherub.

$\frac{3}{4}$ quantity Basic Dough, see page 10
modelling tool
cocktail stick (toothpick)
5cm (2in) heart cutter
1cm ($\frac{1}{2}$in) and 2.5cm (1in) round cutters
small and medium blossom plunger cutters
retracted ballpoint pen
2 Hanging Hooks, see page 17

1   For the legs, roll a little of the dough into two pencil-thin ropes, each about 6cm (2$\frac{1}{2}$in) long. Lay these side by side and trim their ends at a slant: cut the bottoms of the strips so that their longest sides are together; cut the tops so that the shortest sides are together. Make four short cuts in the bottom of each rope to represent toes. Fix the slanting ends at the tops of the ropes together with a little water.
2   Model a small handful of dough into an egg-shaped body. Dampen the back of this and press it, broadest-end down, on the joined tops of the legs. Flatten two very small balls of dough and fix them on the legs to represent

Valentine's Day Mirror

Cherubs and Hearts

CRAFT TIP

The cherubs and hearts are not very difficult to make, so there is no reason why you should not make several, all with different initials . . . just remember not to sign them!

knees. Smooth the edges of the dough into the legs using a damp brush.

3 Roll a suitably sized ball of dough for the head and fit it onto the body. Then roll a tiny ball of dough for a nose and fix it in place.

4 Use a modelling tool to make a wide smiling mouth and give the cherub some cheeks by flattening two small balls of dough on either side of the mouth, smoothing the dough in place as when making the knees. Mark the eyes with a cocktail stick.

5 Make a left arm and a hand to fit the cherub, see page 13, and fix them onto the body, bending the hand above the head. Make the second cherub in the same way, this time

giving him a right hand and arm.

6 Roll out some dough to 6mm ($\frac{1}{4}$in) thick and cut out two hearts. Overlap these slightly, fixing them with a little water.

7 Roll out some more dough to 3mm ($\frac{1}{8}$in) thick. Use the larger round cutter to make about 14 rosebuds, see page 15. Arrange the rosebuds at intervals around the edges of the hearts. Use the small blossom plunger cutter to make small blossoms and attach these between the rosebuds.

8 Shape the letters of your choice from very thin ropes of dough and fix them in the middle of the hearts. Decorate them with a retracted ballpoint pen. Arrange the two cherubs,

134

pressed up against the two hearts and leaning in slightly, with their arms on the outside.

9 Cut out a 25cm (10in) strip of dough. Cut both ends to resemble ribbon. Drape this over the cherubs' heads and bodies, making sure that it passes through their hands. Cut a similar strip of dough and make a bow with tails, see page 13. Fix the bow on the ribbon between the two cherubs' heads, so that the tails drape over the hearts.

10 Model six rosebuds using the smaller round cutter and attach these diagonally across the cherubs' tummies. Use the medium blossom plunger cutter to make flowers to fill in the gaps and add little balls of dough.

11 Fix two short, narrow strips at the ends of each garland to represent ribbons. Arrange some fine, rolled-up ropes of dough on the cherubs' heads to represent curls. Push a hanging hook into the head of each and bake at 145°C (290°F/Gas 1½) for about 1½ hours.

Painting and Finishing

● Float a very thin Rose Pink wash onto the cherubs' cheeks, tummies, knees, fingertips and toes. Mix some Ultramarine and white to a pale blue and paint the initials, blossoms, long ribbon and bow. Quickly mix some white and Rose Pink, and dab a little pale pink onto the blossoms before the blue is completely dry. Paint the garland, roses and ribbons pale pink. Then use pure Rose Pink to paint the roses on the hearts and inside the cherubs' mouths.

When the forget-me-not blossoms and initials are dry, paint each flower centre with a dab of Lemon Yellow and paint the ballpoint indentations on the initials Gold. Continue to use the Gold on the hair and the edges of the ribbon. Add a little pale blue to the eyes.

Paint the tiny circular flowers on the garland white. Add a little white to Olive Green and paint a few leaves on the garland.

· ENGAGEMENT BOWL ·

vegetable oil
ovenproof bowl without lip
1¼ quantities Basic Dough, see page 10
Egg Glaze, see page 11
large heart cutter
about 350 small flat china beads
retracted ballpoint pen
primrose cutter • small heart crimper
medium leaf cutter
2.5cm (1in) round cutter
several stamens

1 Thoroughly oil the outside of the bowl and place it upside down on a baking tray. Take some of the dough and make two thickish ropes long enough to encircle the base of the bowl as it now stands. Make a twist of the two ropes, see page 11, and arrange this around the base. Trim both ends diagonally and join them together neatly with a little water.

2 Roll out half the remaining dough to 6mm (¼in) thick. Cut out sufficient hearts to fit around the bowl on top of the twist. While you still have the hearts loose, dampen the front of them *slightly* with a little egg glaze and press the beads gently into the dough in a heart-shaped design. When you have decorated all the hearts, arrange them around the bowl on top of the twist and with the beads facing inwards. The hearts should be upside down and touching one another. Make sure that you dampen the dough slightly with a little water, where it touches the twist and where the hearts touch each other.

3 Make a finger-thick rope of dough and decorate it with the retracted ballpoint pen before fitting it around the bowl on top of the hearts. Secure it to the points with a little water, decorated side innermost.

CRAFT TIP

The engagement bowl must only be made over the *outside* of an inverted, ovenproof bowl without a rim. Rimmed bowls have a tendency to trap the dough, making it impossible to remove the cooked bowl without ruining all your work.

Pressing beads into the hearts.

Attaching the balls and primroses.

If you wish to use a bowl with a rim or a lip, you must use it the right way up and work *inside* it. This means that you may also arrange the border decoration at the same time, in which case the bowl will only need to go into the oven once.

4   You should be nearing the top of the bowl by now. Make six balls of dough just big enough to stand a little higher than the bottom of the bowl when they are resting on the rope. Attach these with a little water at equal intervals around the bowl.

5   Cut out six primroses and mark their centres with the retracted ballpoint pen. Arrange them in the gaps between the balls. Make a short pencil-thin rope and attach it around the top of the bowl so that it touches the tops of the balls and the flowers.

6   Cut six thin strips of dough and weave them across the top of the bowl, see page 12, securing their ends to the thin rope with a little water. Mark the centre of the outside of each heart with the heart crimper and make a design around the larger single rope with the retracted ballpoint pen. Paint the outside of the bowl with egg glaze. Bake at 145°C (290°F/Gas 1½) for 1½ hours.

7   When the bowl comes out of the oven leave it to cool before removing it from the mould. Then turn it up the right way and decorate the top. Make two doves, see page 15, and secure them on one side of the bowl edge with a little water. Cut out and vein six leaves, see page 16, and arrange them in pairs around the edge at equal intervals from the doves and from each other.

8   Using the 2.5cm (1in) cutter, make three medium roses and place one in the centre of each pair of leaves. Fill the spaces between the roses and doves with flowers made using the primrose cutter. Place three stamens in the centre of each flower. Finally, make a very thin rope and encircle the woven area at the bottom of the bowl with it.

9   Taking care to avoid any areas which you intend to paint, give the bowl a coat of egg glaze and return it to the oven for 1 hour.

Painting and Finishing

● Dampen the leaves with a little clear water. Omitting the tips, paint the leaves with thinned Olive Green. Work diluted Rose Madder into the tips of the leaves so that it blends into the green, see page 19.

Make up a fairly watery mixture of Permanent White and paint the doves. Blend some very thin Ultramarine into their wings and tails and edge them with a little of the diluted Rose Madder. Blend a little of the Rose Madder onto their chests as well and, while you have it on the brush, use it to give a hint of colour to the crimped hearts on the outside of the bowl.

Use the rest of the watery Permanent White to paint the primrose-shaped flowers and edge these with a blend of the Rose Madder.

Thicken the Rose Madder mixture with a little fresh paint and use it to colour the roses, the circle at the bottom of the bowl and the doves' beaks. Mark the doves' eyes with some neat Ultramarine.

As bowls are often used in the kitchen and may be put down on damp surfaces, it is a good idea to give them two or three coats of yacht varnish inside and out.

Engagement Bowl

TEMPLATES

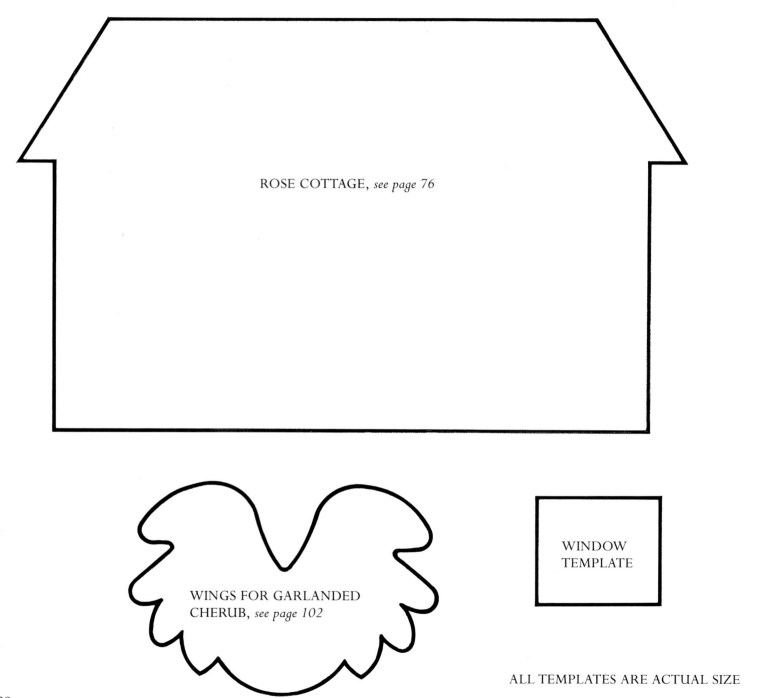

ROSE COTTAGE, *see page 76*

WINGS FOR GARLANDED
CHERUB, *see page 102*

WINDOW
TEMPLATE

ALL TEMPLATES ARE ACTUAL SIZE

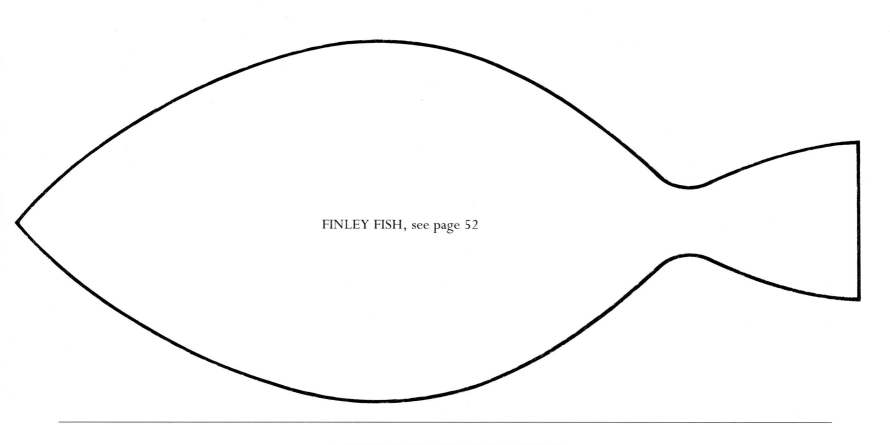

FINLEY FISH, see page 52

ACKNOWLEDGEMENTS

The author and publisher would like to thank the following for assistance in the production of this book.

The Art and Stationery Centre,
15, Tolworth Broadway,
Surbiton,
Surrey.

Blackburns,
Cake Decorating and Craft Equipment,
108, Alexandra Drive,
Surbiton,
Surrey KT5 9AG.

Merehurst is a leading publisher of craft books and has an excellent range of titles to suit all levels. Please send to our address on page 4 for a free catalogue, stating the title of this book.

MARKETING AND SELLING

By the time you reach this part of the book, you will probably be addicted to dough modelling. You will know that this is true when your house and those of friends and relatives bear more than ample evidence of your modelling activities and you find yourself resenting all family meals which have to be cooked in the oven.

You are probably searching frantically for other outlets for dough, both to justify and satisfy your craving for making it, while still retaining the goodwill of friends and family who can only take a certain amount of that kind of thing. The solution, I am happy to say, is simply to sell your work to absolute strangers.

There are several ways of selling your craft, each demanding a different degree of commitment and professionalism. So, before you launch your sales campaign you should consider the options and make a few decisions.

EARNING A LIVING OR MAKING EXTRA CASH

● First decide whether you are looking to earn a living by dough modelling or simply wanting to make some pin-money.
● How much time are you prepared and able to devote to modelling?
● Would the family support your venture?
● Don't forget that it is important to take professional advice on book keeping, tax and car insurance.

SELLING OPTIONS

When you have seriously considered the above points, you will be in a better position to decide how to sell your dough.
● Supply family and friends.
● Take a stall occasionally at a bazaar or fête.
● Sell through shops.
● Set up a party-plan selling scheme.
● Sell through craft fairs.

PRACTICALITIES OF MANUFACTURING AND SELLING

These are the points to clearly define before you attempt to sell dough in any quantity and by any means.

The Range Work out which are your most popular pieces before you start your career as a travelling salesman. This is very important before showing your product. Remember that a shop will want confirmation that the range will stay the same for at least a year and, generally speaking, your price should also remain consistent for at least a year. You can always sneak a seasonal piece or two into the range in addition to the basic items.

Price You must work out a price which is acceptable to you and to the customer. Shop owners have high overheads and it is not fair to expect a shop to pay your normal retail price if you run a party-plan scheme in the area or regularly attend craft fairs, so be prepared to give a shop some discount or you will find that you lose their custom. Many craft workers feel exploited by shop owners and what they consider to be very high mark-ups but if the initial price for the work seemed fair and acceptable, the retail price is entirely up to the shop keeper.

Tot up the cost of flour, salt, paint, varnish, travelling expenses and fuel for baking. If you add on what you consider to be an acceptable hourly rate you can make the product unrealistically expensive. The hard costs must be balanced against non-financial factors such as being your own boss and the luxury of having a fulfilling and flexible lifestyle. Provided that you are neither unduly modest nor arrogant, you should be able to price your work within the average range.

Delivery Dates If anyone decides to give you an order, the first thing he or she will want to clarify is the delivery date. Give yourself a realistic time to complete the order and make sure you always keep to it. Do not be tempted to deliver individual items or groups as they are completed as this wastes time, looks very unprofessional and you probably will not get your money any quicker anyway. Shop owners are likely to want to know if you are prepared to make special orders for customers, so have your answer ready, plus expected delivery times for specials and any extra costs you may wish to charge.

Repeat Orders Make templates of even your most simple designs, especially when making for shops, as customers tend to be finicky about any slight deviation from the norm or from the samples on which they based an order. Make a note of colours as well.

Payment Make a clear set of rules for payment and stick to them – this includes special orders, party-plan selling and selling to shops. Goods should be paid for in full when they are delivered. You may decide to ask for a deposit with special orders or with party-plan selling. The nice part of selling to small shops is that you can insist on cash on delivery because the person who takes the order is usually the owner and the cheque signer too. If this is not the case, telephone a few days in advance of making delivery so that staff know the amount owing and can get the owner organized in time to leave payment for your arrival.

Sale or Return I am not keen on leaving goods on a sale or return basis and neither should you be. If a shop owner is not willing to speculate on a small amount of your dough, then you should take it to someone else who will. If your work is any good someone will be prepared to buy some or you can take it to a craft fair.

Do not be taken in by a shop owner who tries to give you the impression that he or she is doing you a favour by displaying some of your work – it can only bring him or her profit and you could very well lose. Work left on a sale or return basis is often poorly displayed because it has to compete for space with goods which have already been purchased. Your dough can quite literally kick around the shop, deteriorating all the time and becoming less attractive until you eventually have to take it home and throw it away. I cannot see why you or I should finance someone else's business.

SELLING TO FAMILY AND FRIENDS

Initially, the worst aspect of this is the embarrassment of charging and stating your price, particularly if you have been free with your favours previously. Adding up the cost of materials, such as flour, paint, varnish and so on, works wonders for personal business acumen though and it is sure to cure your blushes. At first, you may decide to base the price of your models solely on the cost of the materials; however, if your work is still in demand at this basic cost, you ought to consider something really radical and charge for your time as well!

BAZAARS AND FETES

Generally, this has more to do with self esteem than making money, as these are primarily fund-raising events and you will be expected to contribute part of, if not all, your profit to the cause. It might be worth finding local events, like village fairs, where you are asked to pay a fixed stall fee, then all takings are your own at the end of the day. However, you will have to keep your prices fairly low as many fête-going customers hold very strict views on price control no matter how good the product.

Nevertheless, a bazaar can provide a good setting for your début, particularly if you feel nervous or uncertain about your dough. The feedback from customers will doubtless boost your confidence and their comments can prove more valuable than financial gain at this stage.

SELLING TO SHOPS

The hardest part is actually forcing yourself and your samples through the door – once you have done that, the rest is easy. Most owners run their own craft shops so you will usually find someone behind the counter who can make a decision and give you an order there and then if they like your work.

There are two ways of selling. If you telephone a shop, the chances are the owner has seen a lot of bad work and it is only too easy to put yours into the same category. The excuses for not seeing you are numerous: 'business is bad at the moment, we've tried that before and it didn't sell, we already have a supplier, it's not our kind of thing,' and so on.

It can be difficult to describe dough in glowing terms on the telephone to someone who has never come across it before. For this reason it is often a good idea to present yourself, unannounced, in a shop rather than opting for the more conventional – and polite – way of making an appointment first.

Prepare beforehand and present yourself and your work in an appealing and organized fashion. Avoid calling at very busy times – weekends, bank holidays, Christmas Eve and so on.

PARTY-PLAN SELLING

I did this for a while and I must tell you that it is great fun but very hard work. It may be the scheme for you if you have plenty of stamina and want to make serious money; or more correctly, the scheme for you and a dependable friend because this type of selling calls for a partnership and preferably a dynamic duo!

Decide in advance whether you want to show samples at the party and take orders, or take as much stock as possible and sell it there and then.

Taking Samples If you are taking orders from a sample you can, in effect, sell the same thing over and over again on the same night but you must fix realistic delivery times both for yourself, so that you are not constantly working in a panic, and to maintain the customers' interest. You can always adjust delivery dates to give yourself more time when things start getting busy. If you are doing a lot of parties, your stock will tend to get chipped and broken – wine is often served at these parties, you know – but this does not matter as much when you carry samples as you can explain why they look slightly dog-eared.

Selling Stock In this case, the number of parties has to be limited to the amount of stock which you can produce. As you never know beforehand whether the party is going to be mediocre or a raving success, you should limit yourself to the number of parties you could run if they were all sell outs. The inevitable consequence of not limiting party requests is that you are always in a state of panic, wondering if you are going to have enough stock for the next event and on some occasions almost hoping that you will not sell too much.

Selling and Taking Orders The answer is to compromise. Personalised items, like initials, usually have to be ordered and one or two other items also fall into that sort of category, when the customer will want to stamp her own particular mark on a design. Stock items which are known to be good sellers are probably best sold on the night.

Selling Other Modellers' Work You can take work from other dough modellers and add your own mark up. You must keep accurate records and always give them an itemised receipt as well as being prepared to pay for any breakages.

Organizing the Party It is a good idea to have your first party at home and ask as many people as you can squeeze in. Then, rather than let people wander around at random for the entire evening, as soon as all the guests have arrived, ask for silence and inflict your sales talk on them.

Your presentation should be short and interesting, describing the dough and how it is made. Give a clear idea of what you are offering in the way of designs and service. Finish by mentioning that you are looking for hostesses to give further parties. Plan to offer a cash incentive based on a percentage of the takings or dough to a similar value.

Set a few rules for yourself and your hostess-to-be to avoid the unhappy occurrence of finding yourself making a presentation to a room full of nothing more inspiring than the hostess and her cat. For example, you might decide that you will not hold a party for less than ten guests and then only if they fall within an eight-mile radius of your home. If the hostess is unfortunate enough to live farther away, then she will have to drum up at least fifteen guests. Telephone the hostess two or three days before the event to check that all the conditions are going to be met and that she has remembered that she is having a party!

CRAFT FAIRS

These are a lot of fun and they can provide a reasonable income if you work hard and are careful about the fairs you attend. There are specialist magazines which publish detailed lists of countrywide fairs throughout the year. Fairs advertised in these magazines are usually run by experienced organizers in a professional way. Answers to the following queries should arrive with the booking form, without any prompting from you; however, if information is sparse do not hesitate to telephone the organizer before booking.

● How much and what type of advertising is planned? Ask about newspapers, posters and local radio.

● You should know the number of stalls and the entrance fee. These are related as customers will not pay a high fee for visiting only a handful of stalls.

● Parking facilities are important to you for unloading and to customers who will not bother to stop if parking is in the least bit troublesome.

● There should be signs and banners directing traffic to the venue.

● Is electricity available on your stall?

● Will there be other dough modellers at the fair? One more is acceptable, two are excessive.

● What is the fee for exhibitors? It should include the table and use of electricity but sometimes these things are charged separately.

Stall Fees and Deposits These vary widely depending on how prestigious the venue is and the level of advertising planned. If you have all the relevant information you should be able to judge whether you are likely to get value for money. You usually have to pay a deposit when booking in advance. Most professional craftsmen book for the year and normally pay their deposits by the end of January which is advisable as stalls at good fairs are booked very quickly. When you are first starting, paying several deposits in advance can involve quite a large financial outlay but most organizers will accept post-dated cheques and some of them run schemes which lessen the burden provided that you attend several of their fairs throughout the year.

It is sensible to book yourself into several good fairs over a realistic period of time but always leave sufficient time between fairs to replenish your stock.

Designing Your Stall You will have to do something more enterprising than throwing a cloth over your bare table if you want to sell your wares and impress the organizer. Tables at craft fairs are usually of the folding, trestle type and they tend to measure about 1.8 × 0.75m (6 × 2ft). You cannot rely on this, though, so your display has to be suitable for tables of all sorts of sizes and shapes, as well as being light and capable of folding into nothing in the car. Most people manage to build some kind of display structure from garden trellis which is then fixed to the table using 'G' clamps.

With an attractive cloth, and possibly a canopy over the top, trellis can provide a practical base for hanging dough models. To complete your display you should invest in a couple of clip-on spotlights to highlight your work, and make the paint and varnish sparkle.

INDEX

acrylic paints, 18
animals:
    bears, 15, 55–7, *55*, 99,
        100–101, 106, *106*
    birds, 15
    butterflies, 14
    cats, 14, *53*, 74–5, *75*
    fish, 52–4, *52*, *54*
    hens, 122–5, *123*
    pigs, 50, *51*
    sheep, 49–50, *50–51*
arms, modelling, 13

baking:
    cracks, 23
    sticking problems, 23
    see also under individual projects
'Ballet Dancer Initial', *95*, 92–4
basic dough, 10
baskets, 24–32, *24–33*
'Bear Portraits', 55–7, *55*
bears, 15, 55–7, *55*, 99,
    100–101, 106, *106*
birds, 15
blisters, 23
bowls, 24–32, *24–33*, 135–6,
    137
bows, 13–14, *14*
bread dough, 10–11
    colouring, 11
    drying, 11
    kneading, 11
    quantities, 11
'Bridal Couple', 62–4, *63*
brushes, 18
butterflies, 14

'Candelabra', 125–6, *126*
carnations, 16, *16*
'Carol Singers', 67–71, *69*
'Catherine Sheep', 49–50, *51*
'Cat Napping', *53*, 74–5, *75*
cats, 14, *53*, 74–5, *75*

characters, 46–71
    'Bear Portraits', 55–7, *55*
    'Bridal Couple', 62–4, *63*
    'Carol Singers', 67–71, *69*
    'Catherine Sheep', 49–50, *51*
    'Cat Napping', *53*, 74–5, *75*
    'Claude', *53*, 54
    'Finley Fish', 52–4, *52*
    'George', 47, 48–9
    'Halloween Witch', 57–8, *59*
    'Heathcliffe Pig', 50, *51*
    'Mother and Baby with Pram',
        65–7, *65*
    'Nanny Rabbit and Baby
        Rabbit', 60–62, *61*
    'Victorian Girl', 46–8, *47*
checks, 112
'Cherubs and Hearts', 132–5,
    134
chicken, 122–5, *123*
Christmas decorations, 97–113,
    97–113
    'Christmas Stocking', 105–6,
        106
    'Christmas Teddies', *99*,
        100–101
    'Christmas Tree', *100*
    'Christmas Tree Angel',
        109–11, *109*
    'Christmas Wreath', 41–2, *43*
    'Father Christmas', 98–100,
        99
    'Garlanded Cherub', 102, *103*
    'Gingerbread and Women',
        107–9, *107–8*
    labels, 97–8, *97*
    napkin rings, 117–18, *118*
    'Nativity Scene', 110–13, *111*
    place names, 116–17, *118*
    'Rag Doll Stocking', 106, *106*
    'Rocking Horse', 104–5, *104*
    'Teddy Bear Stocking', 106,
        106

    'Walking Stick', *105*
    'Winged Head Cherub',
        101–2, *103*
Christmas rose, 16
'Claude', *53*, 54
clay guns, 12
cleaning equipment, 8
'Clown Initial', 88–90, *91*
cocktail sticks, 75
colouring, bread dough, 11
cottages, *72–86*, 76–86
cracking, 23
cracks, 8
craft paints, 18
curtains, 74

'Daffodil Bowl', 26–8, *27*
daffodils, 17, *17*
daisies, 16
decorated initials, 87–96, *87–96*
dents, 23
designer colours, 18
discoloured models, 23
dog rose, 16
dots, painting, 19
dough:
    basic, 10
    blisters, 23
    bread, 10–11
    cracking, 23
    hair, 12–13
    painting, 17–22
    paste, 10
    recipes, 8–11
    rolling, 11–12
    twisting, 12
    weaving, 12
doves, 15
drapes, 74
drying, bread dough, 11

'Easter Centrepiece', 114–16, *116*
egg glaze, 11

'Engagement Bowl', 135–6, *137*
'Entwined Hearts', 128, *130*
equipment, 8, *9*
eyes, painting, 19

faces, painting, 18–19, 42
'Father Christmas', 98–100, *99*
feet, modelling, 13
'Festive Table Piece', 118–21,
    119
'Finley Fish', 52–4, *52*
    template, *139*
fish, 52–4, *52*, *54*
    template, *139*
flesh colours, 42
flowers:
    buds, 28
    carnations, 16, *16*
    Christmas rose, 16
    daffodils, 17, *17*, 26–8, *27*
    daisies, 16
    dog rose, 16
    garlands, *37*, 38–9, *39*
    painting, 19
    primroses, 16, 28, *29*
    primulas, 16
    roses, 15
    violets, 16–17, *17*
    wreaths, 34–44, *34–45*
frames, 65
frills, 14, *14*
fruit:
    blackberries, 38
    garlands, 36–8, *36–8*
    strawberries, 30, *31*
    wreaths, 40–1, *40*
'Fruit Bowl', 24–6, *25*

'Garlanded Cherub', 102, *103*
    template, *138*
garlands:
    flowers, *37*, 38–9
    fruit, 36–8, *37*

garlic presses, 12
'George', *47*, 48–9
'Gingerbread Men and Women', 107–9, *107–8*
glazes, egg, 11
gouache, 18

hair, 12–13
'Halloween Witch', 57–8, *59*
hands, modelling, 13, *13*
hanging hooks, 17, 23, 36, 66, 88
hearts, 127–8, 129–30, 132–5, *134*
'Heathcliffe Pig', 50, *51*
hens, 122–5, *123*
holes, hanging, 36, 40
holly wreaths, 41
hooks, 17, 23, 36, 66, 88
'House with a Georgian Door', 78–81, *79*
houses, 72–86, *72–86*
    'House with a Georgian Door', 78–81, *79*
    'Kitchen Dresser', 84–6, *85*
    'Nursery Window', 72–4, *73*
    'Rose Cottage', 76–8, *77*
    'Town House', 81–4, *83*

'Initial with Figure', 90–92, *91*
initials, 87–96, *87–96*
    'Ballet Dancer Initial', *95*, 92–4
    'Clown Initial', 88–90, *91*
    'Initial with Figure', 90–92, *91*
    'Tennis Player Initial', *91*, 94–6
    'Twisted Floral Initial', 87–8, *89*

'Kitchen Dresser', 84–6, *85*
kneading, 8
    bread dough, 11
    salt dough, 11

labels, Christmas, 97–8, *97*
'Lady in Blue', 108
'Lady in Green', 108
leaves, 15–16, *15*
legs, modelling, 13
letters, 87–96, *97–6*
'Love Birds Heart', 127–8, *129*

'Man with the Moustache', 108
'Man in the Tartan Jacket', 108
marketing, 140–42
menorah, 125–6
mirrors, 131–2, *133*
modelling, 13–14, *13–14*
'Mother and Baby with Pram', 65–7, *65*
'Mother Hen', 122–5, *123*
'Mother's Day Dish', 32, *33*

'Nanny Rabbit and Baby Rabbit', 60–62, *61*
'Nativity Scene', 110–13, *111*
'Nursery Window', 72–4, *73*

ovenproof dish technique, 24, *24*

painting, 17–22
    dots, 19
    faces, 18–19
    flower patterns, 19
    patterns, 19
    projects, 20–22
    spots, 19
    tartans, 19
    terms, 18
paints, 17–18
paste dough, 10
patterns, painting, 19
pigeons, 15
pigs, 50, *51*
place names, 116–17, *118*
poster paints, 18
'Primrose Basket', 28, *29*

primroses, 16, 28, *29*
primulas, 16

'Rag Doll Stocking', 106, *106*
robins, 15
'Rocking Horse', 104–5, *104*
rolling ropes, 11–12
romantic messages, 127–36, *127–37*
    'Cherubs and Hearts', 132–5, *134*
    'Engagement Bowl', 135–6, *137*
    'Entwined Hearts', 128, *130*
    'Love Birds Heart', 127–8, *129*
    'Valentine's Day Mirror', 131–2, *133*
ropes:
    rolling, 11–12
    splitting, 23
    twists, 12
rosebuds, 15
'Rose Cottage', 76–8, *77*
    template, 138
roses, 15

salt dough:
    modelling techniques, 11–12
    recipe, 10
selling, 140–42
sheep, 49–50, *50–51*
sieves, 13
spots, painting, 19
'Strawberry Basket', 30, *31*
stripes, 112
sugarcraft cutters, 8

table decorations, 114–26, *114–26*
    'Candelabra', 125–6, *126*
    'Christmas Napkin Rings', 117–18, *118*

'Christmas Place Names', 116–17
'Easter Centrepiece', 114–16, *116*
'Festive Table Piece', 118–21, *119*
'Mother Hen', 122–5, *123*
'Thanksgiving Sheaf', 121–2, *121*

tartans, painting, 19
'Teddy Bear Stocking', 106, *106*
teddy bears, 15, *15*, 55–7, *55*, 99, 100–101, 106, *106*
templates, 138–9
'Tennis Player Initial', *91*, 94–6
'Thanksgiving Sheaf', 121–2, *121*
'Thanksgiving Wreath', 42–4, *45*
toothpicks, 75
'Town House', 81–4, *83*
'Twisted Floral Initial', 87–8, *89*
twists, 12

'Valentine's Day Mirror', 131–2, *133*
varnishing, 17, 18, 52
'Victorian Girl', 46–8, *48*
'Victorian Wreath', 34–6, *35*
violets, 16–17, *17*

'Walking Stick', *105*
water colours, 17–18
weaving, 12
windows, *53*, 72–4, *72–4*, 74–6, *74–5*
    template, 138
'Winged Head Cherub', 101–2, *103*
witches, 57–8, *59*
wreaths, 34–44, *34–45*
    Christmas, 41–2, *43*
    flower, 34–44, *34–45*
    fruit, 40–1, *40*
    Thanksgiving, 42–4, *45*
    Victorian, 34–6, *35*